Slumps, Grunts, and Snickerdoodles

What Colonial America Ate and Why

QUEBEC

NEW ENGLAND

NEW YORK

PENNSYLVANIA

NEW JERSEY

MARYLAND

VIRGINIA

NORTH CAROLINA

SOUTH CAROLINA

GEORGIA

FLORIDA

Adapted from a British military map of 1767

Slumps, Grunts, and Snickerdoodles

What Colonial America Ate and Why ✳ **Lila Perl**

drawings by

✳ *Richard Cuffari*

Clarion Books / New York

Clarion Books
a Houghton Mifflin Company imprint
215 Park Avenue South, New York, NY 10003
Text copyright © 1975 by Lila Perl
Illustrations copyright © 1975 by Houghton Mifflin Company
Designed by Victoria Gomez

Printed in the USA
Library of Congress Cataloging in Publication Data
Perl, Lila.
  Slumps, grunts and snickerdoodles:
what Colonial America ate and why.
  Includes index.
  SUMMARY: Examines the diets and culinary
innovations of the American colonists and gives
thirteen colonial recipes, including succotash,
snickerdoodles, and spoon bread.
  1. Cookery, American—Juvenile literature.
[1. Cookery. 2. United States—Social life and
customs—Colonial period, ca. 1600-1775]
I. Cuffari, Richard, 1925-   ill. II. Title.
TX15.P469   641.5'973   75-4894
ISBN 0-395-28923-8

VB   20 19 18 17 16 15 14

Acknowledgments

Quotations used in the text are from the following:

Beverly, Robert. *History and Present State of Virginia.* Louis B. Wright, ed. Chapel Hill: University of North Carolina Press, 1947.

Bradford, William. *Of Plymouth Plantation 1620–1647.* Samuel Eliot Morison, ed. New York: Alfred A. Knopf, Inc., 1952.

Byrd, William. *The Writings of "Colonel William Byrd of Westover in Virginia, Esqr."* J. S. Bassett, ed. New York, 1901.

Percy, George. *A Discourse of the Plantation of the Southern Colonie in Virginia.* 1607.

Smith, John, and others. *The Generall Historie of Virginia.* Compiled by William Simons, 1624.

Contents

Between the Discoveries and the Revolution

It took hundreds of years, between Columbus's discovery of the New World and the signing of the Declaration of Independence, for the United States of America to be born. Although the Spanish established the first permanent settlement in what is today the U.S.A.—at St. Augustine, Florida, in 1565—we usually think of the "colonial" period as having begun with the first permanent British settlement, at Jamestown, Virginia, in 1607.

Political events, legal proclamations, and battle dates are really the bare bones of history. The one hundred and seventy years during which the thirteen colonies of North America's eastern seaboard, from New Hampshire in the north to Georgia in the south, grew and prospered, were a period of rich and vibrant social development. The ferment of cultures—American Indian, British, Dutch, German, African, and West Indian—bubbled and blended, producing new manners and customs, new types of dwellings and clothing, new occupations and patterns of daily living. The ferment also produced new methods of cookery, new cooking ingredients and food combinations—in fact, a whole new cuisine.

The social history of colonial America can be explored with astonishing success in terms of those often oddly-named dishes that steamed, simmered, boiled, and baked in the fireplaces. In this book, thirteen colorfully titled recipes have been chosen to tell not only *what* the colonists ate and *why*, but to show the geographical and historical background as well as the intimate domestic surroundings in which these developments took place.

If the names of the recipes are uniformly mysterious and confusing—corn oysters and hush puppies, spoon bread, snickerdoodles, and johnnycake, country captain and tipsy squire—this is because each is a clue to some facet of colonial life in the diverse New England, Middle Atlantic, and Southern settlements of the 17th and 18th centuries, and by each recipe there hangs a tale.

In unlocking the secrets behind short'nin' bread and shoo-fly pie, in probing the parentage of Indian pudding and apple pandowdy, in unraveling the reasons for red-flannel hash and succotash, we will find that we can evoke and examine a vivid segment of our rapidly disappearing past.

Age, however, has not dulled the taste or dimmed the appearance of these thirteen recipes. Presented in their authentic form, with only occasional helpful modifications for modern cooks, these dishes are every bit as good in contemporary meals as when they were eaten off the rough board tables of our colonial forefathers.

Perhaps the greatest reward, beyond the joy of having discovered at firsthand the dishes that brought colonial families together for moments of warmth and cheer in a harsh and often hostile environment, is that of having pieced together into a whole fabric the many elements that not only shaped our heritage but have deeply influenced the American here-and-now.

The New England Colonies

It All Began with Indian Corn

A hideous and desolate wilderness, full of wild beasts and wild men."

This was how William Bradford, who later became governor of Plymouth Colony, described the coast of North America when the Pilgrims first touched shore at Cape Cod in November of 1620.

After two months of sailing on rough seas, in a cramped and wave-tossed vessel, the *Mayflower* passengers were seeking a less bleak and hopeless-looking landing place.

But before they pushed on, along the coast of Cape Cod Bay, they explored the harbor region near the tip of the Cape. There they came by accident upon their first encouraging sign in the New World—a field of stubble where Indian corn had been planted and reaped in the summer just past.

In his detailed journal, *Of Plymouth Plantation*, covering the years 1620 to 1647, Bradford tells how the Pilgrims discovered, quite near the cornfield, heaps of sand in which were buried Indian baskets filled with corn, "some in ears, fair and good, of divers colours, which seemed to them a very goodly sight (having never seen any such before)."

One month later, in December of 1620, the Pilgrims made their decision to settle permanently at Plymouth, directly across Cape Cod Bay. The site they chose had been an Algonquian Indian village until 1617 when it was abandoned because of a smallpox epidemic. The village clearing lay close to a high hill that lent itself to fortification. But the main attractions of this deserted place were its clear running brooks and its promising fields that had once yielded up Indian corn. These features, in Bradford's words, made Plymouth "a place fit for situation."

Of course, the Pilgrims intended at the time to plant their own seeds of wheat, oats, rye, barley, and peas in the empty Indian cornfields. They did not know that much of their seed had rotted on the long, damp journey from England. Nor did they realize that they had come to the land of Indian corn, to an entire continent in fact where no European grains—no wheat or oats, no rye or barley—had ever been heard of before the first visits of European ships and sailors.

Similarly, Indian corn was unknown in Europe and elsewhere around the globe before the discovery and investigation of the New World by European explorers, traders, and fishermen.

The Norsemen, who visited the eastern shores of North America from time to time between about A.D. 1000 and 1347, noted the existence of Indian corn but do not appear to have written anything or spread much information about it after returning home. Possibly they did not realize the importance of this grain throughout the Americas, as it was grown in relatively small quantities by the Indians of the coastal New England region that the Norsemen called Vinland.

However, a group of Columbus's men, exploring the island of Cuba in November 1492, enthusiastically reported finding "a sort of grain called *mahiz*" that could be eaten as a cereal or ground into flour. The word *mahiz* was from the Taino language, the aboriginal tongue spoken by the local island people. In Spanish it became *maiz* and in English, maize.

This, then, was the first important word from the Americas about the strange new food plant. In Europe, maize was widely dubbed "Indian corn" so as not to be confused with the word corn as it had been used from ancient times in Europe, Asia, and Africa. Corn, in the general sense, had always referred to the important grain or grains of a particular country. It could mean the wheat and barley of ancient Egypt or the oats of sixteenth-century Scotland. To more clearly distinguish this newly found member of the family of cereal grasses, botanists labeled Indian corn *Zea mays*.

When, where, and how did Indian corn begin? Like other food plants grown by man, it began as a wild grass. Maize probably appeared first in tropical or subtropical America, long before the Indians migrated to the Americas from Asia. In 1953, archeological diggings in Mexico City revealed the existence of fossilized corn pollen grains believed to be 60,000 to 80,000 years old. This is the earliest record we have of the corn plant, growing wild, in America, and we can probably assume that parts of it were food for wild animals.

Once the Indians (who migrated to the Americas about

20,000 years ago) learned to plant corn for food, a number of varieties and colors, shapes and sizes, developed as a result of cross-fertilizing the pure-strain plants. The oldest domesticated corncobs found were a tiny thumb-size variety, discovered in the refuse remains of early Indian cave-dwellers near Puebla, Mexico. The cobs are believed to date from 5200 B.C.

By the time the Pilgrims appeared on the scene, corn had become the very basis of a number of advanced Indian civilizations. The Aztecs of Mexico, the Mayas of Central America, and the Incas of Peru could never have prospered without a large well-fed populace. But the maize of the newly discovered Americas hardly resembled the sweet, delicate, white or golden ears that most of us are familiar with today. Indian corn came in a bewildering array of colors and patterns, with kernels that might be red or pink, blue, brown, or black, striped, swirled, or spotted. The kernels ranged in size from smaller than a grain of rice to larger than a lima bean.

The Algonquian Indians, who inhabited the region of North America that was later to be called New England, did not rank very high among the Indian agriculturalist peoples of their day. Their farming was limited, in part, by the severe winters and the short growing season. They led a relatively primitive existence, and their numbers remained small over the centuries. They subsisted largely on game and river fish and on shellfish dug from the coastal beaches. Each summer they grew enough corn to supply their needs until the next year's harvest was due.

Having no metal tools, horses, or wheeled vehicles for plowing, they used the simplest possible method for planting. They fashioned the soil into small hills or into mounded rows and dropped the seed into the softened earth. Seeds of beans, squash, and pumpkin, all of which were native to the Americas, were planted in the same fashion as corn. These vegetables, along with sunflowers, which were grown for the oil in their seeds, were almost the only food plants cultivated by the Indians of the northeast. Yet they proved to be the means of survival for the Pilgrims who settled at Plymouth in that dreary December of 1620.

The first terrible months of 1621 saw the deaths of 50 of the 102 *Mayflower* passengers. But spring came at last, bringing hope in the person of Squanto, an English-speaking Algonquian who had been taken to Britain by British fishermen six or seven years earlier and who had returned to his ravaged people following the smallpox epidemic of 1617.

So, the "wild men" of whom Bradford had despaired produced sympathetic and helpful individuals: Samoset, who first introduced Squanto to the Pilgrim band, the friendly chief Massasoit who kept a peace treaty with the Plymouth settlers until his death in 1661, and of course Squanto himself.

It was from Squanto that the settlers learned how to plant the corn, beans, pumpkin, and squash for their first harvest, which culminated in the Thanksgiving feast of autumn 1621. And from the "wild men" they also learned how to turn the "wild beasts" of Bradford's "hideous and desolate wilderness" to their advantage. The former town-dwelling artisans and tradesmen were taught how to hunt successfully for venison and bear, how to dig the sandy beaches for the hard-shelled clam known as the quahog, and how to pluck spawning fish out of the swift-running rivers. In

teaching the Pilgrims the planting of corn, Squanto instructed them in the ancient Indian technique of fertilizing their maize patches by burying one of the plentiful fish of the herring family, such as a shad or an alewife, in each seed hillock.

However, the wheat and peas, brought from England, seemed to adapt poorly to the new soil and climate. "Some English seed they sowed, as wheat and pease," Governor Bradford wrote, of the crops the Pilgrims planted in the spring of 1621, "but it came not to good, either by the badness of the seed or lateness of the season or both, or some other defect."

So Indian corn was to be the mainstay of the Pilgrims of Plymouth Colony, of the Puritans who founded Massachusetts Bay Colony at Salem in 1628, and of the other early colonists of New England. Later, after some experimentation in adapting the proper seed strains to the soil and climate, wheat was grown more successfully. But the New England landscape, hilly and stony, lacked the broad rolling spaces for large wheatfields, and corn continued to come to the dinner table in one form or another for many years. Not surprisingly, corn was the principal ingredient in most of the early New England recipes.

Today we think of wheat rather than corn as being the principal agricultural crop of the United States. Yet corn, the native American grain, has never lost its prominence. As many as 5.7 billion bushels of corn are produced annually in the United States as against 1.7 billion bushels of wheat; the United States produces over 50 percent of the corn in the world today. Corn is also grown in quantity, as a popular table food in Russia, Romania, Italy, and Yugoslavia, as well as throughout Africa, in mainland China, and, of course, in Canada and Latin America.

Cornbread, cornmeal mush, and succotash may not appear on American dinner tables as frequently as they did in colonial times, but corn reaches us just the same. About 85 percent of the American corn crop is used to feed the hogs, cattle, chickens, and other livestock that we eat. The balance of the crop that is used for food appears as fresh, canned, or frozen corn, as cornmeal and hominy, as snacks, confections, and breakfast cereals such as cornflakes, as cornstarch, corn syrup, corn oil, and as corn mash which is used to make the native American distilled spirit known as bourbon whiskey. Industrially, corn oil turns up in paints and soaps, corn proteins in synthetic fibers, adhesives, and explosives, cornstarch in fabrics, leather, and paper, and even the cornstalks are used, in building and packing materials.

In looking back to the foundation of North America's agricultural wealth, its industrial development, its cookery traditions and its present-day eating patterns, even its very culture and civilization, it would certainly not be wrong to say that it all began with Indian corn.

Succotash
A Stew from the Stalk

✳ With all the elk, moose, and deer, the pheasants and partridges, wild ducks, geese, and turkeys, the fish and shellfish available to the early New England colonists, it may seem strange to us that they so craved cereal grains and vegetable foods in their diet. But we must remember that these former English townspeople and small farmers were unused to the high protein diet of the American Indian hunter and woodsman and that they longed to recreate as many of the dishes of home as possible.

At first, of course, they lacked the necessary ingredients. Just as there was no English wheat for bread, there were no English peas for a fresh cooked vegetable in summer or for a dried-pea "pease pudding" in winter. The pea plant, native to southwestern Asia, had over the course of centuries traveled to Europe where it had become popular in England. But in the New World there simply were no peas when the first settlers arrived.

There were, however, beans—beans of many more sizes,

shapes, colors, and flavors than the Old World had ever known. Asia of course had the soy bean, and in Europe the broad bean was the most common. But in the Americas the Indians all the way from Canada to near the tip of South America grew numerous types of beans.

Most of these had originated in South and Central America and some had traveled to northeastern America so that the Indians of New England had red kidney beans, white pea beans (also called navy beans), red cow peas (really beans), and other types that were given names like "soldier" beans and "yellow-eye" beans by the colonists.

The Indians had the easiest method in the world for growing beans. They simply planted the bean seeds in the soil beside the sprouting corn. Then, as the bean vines grew, they entwined themselves around the tall-growing stalks of corn. When both corn and beans were ripe for harvesting, the corn kernels and the shelled beans were cooked in water and then flavored with nut, fish, or sunflower oil, or perhaps with a thick coating of the bear grease that the New England Indian liked on his food. For winter eating, the corn and beans could be preserved for long-keeping by drying and could then be cooked and served up in similar fashion.

This Indian dish of corn and beans was called *sukquitta-hash*. It was one of the first, the simplest, and the most directly adopted recipes taken from the Indians by the colonists.

There were, of course, a few changes made in the dish as time went by. Once dairy cattle arrived in New England (within a couple of years after the Pilgrims' arrival), milk or cream, and butter, were added to the cooked corn and beans instead of the more pungently flavored animal fats that the

Indians used. The colonists also discovered that an excellent one-dish meal could be produced by adding bits of game or, later on, chunks of corned beef, chicken, and salt pork to the corn and beans.

Turnips, rutabagas, and carrots, which the colonists were soon growing, also went nicely in this dish. And after potatoes began to be grown in New England (around 1719 in New Hampshire), they too were added. Although native to South America, the white potato actually had to go to Europe to become popularized and was reintroduced to the New World by Scotch-Irish immigrants to New England.

Another South American touch was later provided by the lima bean which became a replacement for the white pea bean that the first settlers put into the dish. And, of course, even before most of these changes in ingredients had taken place, the name of the dish had been simplified from *sukquttahash* to succotash!

So traditional is succotash that it is still eaten in New England every year on Forefathers' Day, celebrated on December 21 to commemorate the Pilgrims' landing on Plymouth Rock in 1620. The type of succotash eaten on this day is the wintertime main-dish version, with meat, poultry, and root vegetables added to the dried pea beans and dried corn—and it is suitably named Plymouth succotash. Forefathers' Day has been observed in New England since 1769.

The beans of the New World also provided a number of substantial and nourishing dishes all on their own. It is no accident that Boston baked beans became the hallmark of New England eating. Boston, which was settled in 1630 by Puritans of the Massachusetts Bay Colony, was a deeply religious community. Preparation for the carefully observed

Sunday Sabbath, on which prayer was the only activity permitted, made Saturday an especially busy day for the New England housewife. So, early in the morning, she set a pot of pea beans flavored with onion, salt pork, and molasses into the slow-baking fireplace oven to be ready in time for Saturday night's supper.

Returning to succotash, New England's earliest "stew from the stalk," here is the recipe for a traditional-style succotash prepared with dried pea beans and dried corn, along with a more modern version of succotash using lima beans.

❋ SUCCOTASH

½ cup uncooked dried white pea beans
¾ cup dried sweet corn (whole kernels), or
     1½ cups canned whole-kernel corn, well-drained
2 tablespoons butter or margarine
¾ cup cold milk
2 tablespoons flour
1 teaspoon salt
⅛ teaspoon white pepper
½ teaspoon sugar

• Wash dried pea beans and dried corn separately, by rinsing each well in a strainer. Place each in a bowl with enough cold water to completely cover the contents, and let soak overnight.

• Next day, place each in a medium-size saucepan, add additional water to cover, bring to a boil, reduce heat, and simmer with lid on until tender. Dried corn will take 30 to

45 minutes; dried beans will take 1 hour or more. Drain well.

• In a medium-large saucepan, melt the butter. Combine milk and flour until perfectly smooth. Add to butter in saucepan and cook over medium-high heat, beating constantly with a wire whisk, until mixture is thickened. Add salt, pepper, and sugar. Add cooked corn and beans. (If using canned corn, add it as is at this point in place of the prepared dried corn.)

• Blend succotash ingredients, heat through gently until hot, without boiling, and serve.

• This is a "winter" succotash. For a summer-type succotash, substitute 1½ cups cooked fresh or frozen corn and 1½ cups cooked fresh or frozen lima beans. Serves 6.

Johnnycake
Travelin' Bread

✳ Corn and beans, pumpkin and squash, partridge and rabbit might do very well to fill the fireplace cooking pot, but the overriding desire of the early New England settlers was for bread, bread as similar as possible to the yeast-raised wheaten loaves of Europe.

Bread, of course, required flour, and while wheat flour could not be obtained at first in the New World, it was possible to grind dried corn into a very fine meal that resembled a coarse flour.

The Indians had been doing just this for centuries. The trying task of converting whole corn kernels into particles or cornmeal had somehow been designated as women's work among the Indians of the northeast. And a never-ending job it was, standing over a hollowed-out tree trunk pounding away for hours at the hard, dry contents within with a heavy wooden club until the beaten corn was fine enough for making samp or pone.

Samp and pone (Indian words that the early colonists

soon adopted) were really the Indians' "breads." Samp was a porridge of cornmeal and water, cooked to a lumpy thickness over an open fire, while pone was a small rounded or oval cake of cornmeal with just enough water added to make the grains stick together.

The molded cake was then placed in the hot ashes of the fire and baked. It was always a little gritty and cindery but to the first settlers it seemed the nearest thing to bread, as they knew it, and they were determined to try to improve it with the addition of yeast, milk, sugar and salt, and thus bake it into a proper loaf—high, light, and crusty.

The first attempt to bake a "raised" loaf of cornbread must have caused bafflement and despair among the New England settlers. For the yeast did not perform its usual action of puffing up the dough mixture to at least double its size, and after the cornbread was baked in the fireplace oven with care, it came out looking just as flat and tasting just as crumbly-textured as the crudely baked corn pone of the Indians.

What the colonists did not know at the time was that, unlike wheat and (to some degree) rye flour, cornmeal contains no gluten, the elastic protein substance that makes wheat-flour doughs sticky and stretchy. When yeast releases its gas into a sticky dough mixture, small air-filled cells are formed and the entire mass enlarges. But when gas is released into a cornmeal mixture, it cannot be captured and therefore makes its way out into the surrounding air.

So the colonists' hopes fell as flat as their cornmeal bread and they were soon back to baking Indian pone, improving the flavor somewhat by adding salt and sugar, milk and butter, and baking their bread on a greased fireplace griddle,

pancake fashion, to avoid the gritty coating it acquired when baked directly in the ashes.

Another change that quickly came about was the method of grinding the cornmeal itself. New England was full of small but powerful gushing streams and waterfalls. By the 1630s the Indian-style samp mortars, as they were called, were being replaced by gristmills, with millstones that were kept turning by a water-powered wheel.

One of the great advantages of Indian-style pone was that it could be baked quickly, even at a wayside campfire if need be. Also, it traveled well. A "pancake" of cold cornmeal bread could be carried in one's saddlebag to be toasted over a fire for good on-the-move eating. If it could be slathered with butter or maple syrup while hot, or dipped in a stew gravy, so much the better. These cornmeal cakes came to be quite popular with the early traveling preachers and judges who did their rounds of duty in the scattered New England settlements, and it was not long before their traveling bread got to be known as "journey cake."

In Rhode Island, which was becoming famous for its exceedingly fine, white, waterground cornmeal, the name "journey cake" somehow slid into "jonnycake." Other places picked up the word and, assuming it had something to do with the name John (which it did not), inserted the "h," making it "johnnycake."

Today the name "journey cake" has virtually disappeared, while "johnnycake" remains in fairly common use. Rhode Island, however, continues to hold fast to "jonnycake"—no "h"—and to use only white cornmeal in its recipe, although white *or* yellow is perfectly acceptable everywhere else!

Little by little, other grains began to creep into baked cornmeal products, adding new flavors and textures, and pleasing the palates of the bread-hungry colonists. "Rye 'n Injun" was the name of one early improvement. It contained a mixture of rye flour and cornmeal. Rye was a grain that took to the New England soil more readily than wheat.

Boston brown bread, which became the traditional accompaniment to Saturday night baked beans, was so good it was almost a pudding. It called for about equal quantities of cornmeal, wheat, and rye flour, and it was sweetened with molasses and sometimes raisins. It was originally prepared by steaming, in an English-style pudding bag, and is nowadays baked in covered cylindrical molds or in coffee cans so that it is moist and springy and the slices are always round.

And then there was anadama bread, a cornmeal and wheat bread that actually had enough wheat flour in it to be raised by yeast. The story behind anadama bread is that there was once a New England fisherman who grew exceedingly tired of the cornmeal mush served up for dinner day after day by his unimaginative wife, Anna. Adding several fistfuls of wheat flour, some yeast, and some molasses to Anna's mush, he set the entire mess to rise, baked it, and ate the hot delicious loaf, while muttering angrily to himself between satisfying mouthfuls, "Anna, damn her!"

Even though the improved wheaten loaves continued to gain popularity as time went by, the New England colonists never forgot the early versions of Indian corn pone that saw them through the first days, months, and years in the New World. Here is a recipe for johnnycake as it might have been prepared in seventeenth-century New England.

✳ JOHNNYCAKE

1 cup yellow or white cornmeal
¾ teaspoon salt
2 teaspoons sugar
1 cup water
2 tablespoons butter
¼ cup milk
   butter, or margarine, and oil for frying
   butter or margarine for topping
   maple or pancake syrup

• Measure cornmeal, salt, and sugar into a medium-size mixing bowl. Measure water and the 2 tablespoons butter into a medium-small saucepan and heat to a rolling boil.

• Immediately pour hot mixture over cornmeal mixture, in a slow trickle, stirring constantly. When butter has melted and all liquid has been absorbed, add milk. Mixture should be fairly thick.

• Heat a large griddle or skillet. Add butter, or margarine, and oil in about equal quantities and spread them around to cover the entire surface generously. When fat is sizzling, drop johnnycake batter onto skillet from a large tablespoon, forming cakes that are about 4 inches in diameter. When golden-brown and crisp on underside, lift carefully with a broad-edged spatula or pancake turner, and turn and brown other side.

• Serve cakes hot from griddle, topped with additional butter and with maple or pancake syrup. Johnnycake is good at breakfast time. It can also be eaten at dinner with meat and gravy. Makes 12 4-inch cakes.

Indian Pudding
English Dessert, American Style

✳ Almost every happy memory the New England colonists had of their former life in England revolved around some festive occasion, one that was often celebrated with a rich pudding.

The most gala pudding of all was plum pudding, although oddly enough this dish did not contain any plums. It did include, however, all sorts of choice imported tidbits (referred to as "plums") such as raisins and dried currants, almonds and candied orange peel. Its base was suet, or beef fat, and flour, and it usually was served with a "hard sauce" of cold, beaten butter, sugar, and brandy, and often set aflame with brandy as well.

During their early years in the New World, the colonists could only dream of the plum puddings of Old England. Even a simple milk pudding or bread pudding seemed out of the question because of the absence of wheat flour. But there was, of course, Indian cornmeal.

The very first pudding the New England settlers managed to throw together was called hasty pudding. It consisted of water and cornmeal boiled together until thick and was only a little different from Indian samp porridge in that it was sweetened with molasses, or maple sugar or honey, and sometimes had a lump of butter tossed into it for added richness and flavor.

With the increase in the number of dairy cattle brought to Plymouth Colony from England during the late 1620s, milk and milk products became somewhat more plentiful and the Pilgrims could begin to approach the idea of an English-style milk pudding. Wheat flour was still scarce, of course, so they used cornmeal instead and called the new creamy, baked dessert "Indian" pudding, even though it contained such non-Indian ingredients as milk, eggs, butter, molasses for sweetening, and pinches of such exotic spices as cinnamon and ginger. Thick cream, when available, was poured over the pudding—another non-Indian and distinctly English touch.

The molasses that went into the New England Indian pudding was a special case, for it was neither British nor American Indian in origin. It was the product of Yankee business enterprise as expressed through the New England sea trade.

As early as 1492, Columbus saw the possibility of growing sugarcane on the moist tropical islands of the West Indies. On his second voyage to the New World he brought along slips of the sugarcane plant which had originated in ancient times in India and had been grown for hundreds of years in Spain. By the time New England was being colonized, the sugar plantations of the Western hemisphere were flourishing, exporting refined sugar to Europe and importing slaves from Africa to work the sugar fields.

Perched on the rocky seacoast of eastern North America, the colonists soon saw their chance to carve out a trading pattern of their own by sailing down to the West Indies with timber and dried fish, and returning with molasses, the sweet thick brown liquid that was the cheap by-product of sugar manufacture.

By the second half of the seventeenth century, much of the molasses that was unloaded at Boston harbor was being thriftily converted into the alcoholic beverage, rum, at New England distilleries. Rum, in turn, was exported to Africa where it was exchanged for shipments of slaves to grow more sugar in the West Indies.

Thus the molasses that went into New England's baked beans and Indian puddings, that sweetened its mince and pumpkin pies, and that was poured onto its hasty pudding and over its slabs of fried cornmeal mush (prepared from thick slices of cold hasty pudding) was but one element in a highly profitable three-way trading cycle. And while the imported molasses may have united New England families in the pleasures of the table, the system that produced it condemned slave families to lives of disruption and despair.

Although hasty pudding and even Indian pudding became fairly common desserts in New England, holiday time was naturally the period when molasses for sweet desserts was in highest demand. As the Puritans, in particular, refused to celebrate Christmas because of their rebellion against the Church of England and its religious customs, Thanksgiving—the totally American holiday—became the principal American festival. If there was a mince pie or a rich raisin-studded Indian pudding (reminiscent of an English plum pudding) to be served, it was presented at a family's Thanksgiving feast. It is a matter of historical

record that if a shipment of molasses from the West Indies was late, due to a foundering ship or a storm at sea, a New England town would casually put off its Thanksgiving celebration for a week or two, or even for a month, until the missing ingredient arrived!

Indian pudding is an excellent example of the kinds of hybrid recipes that developed in the New World. It is the true offspring of English memories and American wilderness realities. Here is the recipe for a medium-rich Indian pudding. Such a pudding might have been served in Boston, in the late 1600s, as the dessert at a Saturday night supper of baked beans, brown bread, and pickles.

✳ INDIAN PUDDING

2½ cups milk
 3 tablespoons cornmeal
 ½ cup molasses
 2 tablespoons butter
 2 eggs
 ½ teaspoon ground cinnamon
 ¼ teaspoon ground ginger
    pinch salt

• Set oven to heat to 300 degrees Fahrenheit.

• Pour the milk into a medium-large saucepan and heat over medium-high heat just until the milk is scalded (tiny bubbles will appear around the edge). Watch carefully so that milk does not boil.

• Add cornmeal, one tablespoon at a time, stirring after each addition to prevent lumps from forming. Add molasses and butter. Reduce heat under saucepan to low and cook mixture 10 to 15 minutes, stirring frequently, until thickened.

• In a medium-size mixing bowl, beat eggs with a wire whisk. Add cinnamon, ginger, and salt. Slowly add hot cornmeal mixture to egg mixture, beating constantly with whisk.

• Butter a one-quart casserole or other deep baking dish. Pour mixture into casserole and bake at 300 degrees for 45 minutes.

• Serve Indian pudding warm. Heavy cream may be poured over the top. Although not traditional, a scoop of vanilla ice cream is an especially good topping for a portion of Indian pudding. Serves 4–6.

Corn Oysters
Thinking Fish

✳ In New England, fish was just naturally uppermost on everybody's mind. The Indians had long been eating fish and shellfish from the rivers, lakes, and sandy-shored coastal bays. In fact, they found this major item of their diet to be so plentiful upon their very doorstep that they never even bothered to build ocean-going vessels with which to go out to sea and catch fish.

Fishing was what first drew Norsemen from Scandinavia, Frenchmen from Brittany, and other European seamen to the eastern shores of North America. Between 1600 and 1620, before the Pilgrims set down roots at Plymouth, the New England coast had been visited quite often by British fishermen who sometimes camped ashore in summer to salt and dry their catch.

And of course the Pilgrims themselves, soon after their arrival, began to taste the bounty of clams and oysters, mussels and scallops, lobster and cod offered along the coast or just a few miles offshore.

The famed New England clambake developed very early in the colonial period. It was nothing more than an adaptation of the coastal Indians' method of cooking clams in a pit lined with seaweed, which provided moisture for steaming the clams. Over the years, the New Englanders added the lobsters, corn, and potatoes, and of course the salt, pepper, and hot dripping butter that made the succulent clambake food so delicious.

By the 1630s the New England colonists were putting out to sea for cod, and the first half of the 1700s saw the growth of fishing fleets and the development of Massachusetts ports like Gloucester and Marblehead as centers of fishing and fish-processing. Cod was the basis of the dried-fish trade with the West Indies, and it was also the basis of the hot, crusty codfish balls that Bostonians ate for breakfast on Sunday mornings and the hearty cod chowder and boiled cod dinners that filled hungry bellies at mealtime everywhere on the windswept coast.

While dried salted cod was the staple food, useful for codfish cakes and balls, chowders, stews, and hashes, the scarcer fresh cod was the food chosen for festive occasions by coastal New Englanders who sometimes celebrated with a dish they called "Cape Cod turkey." It consisted of a huge baked, stuffed codfish surrounded with all the fixings that would ordinarily appear at a grand turkey dinner farther inland where game was more available than fish.

Unlike cod, haddock, and other plentiful ocean fish, shellfish did not lend itself to salting and drying, or to other preserving methods known at the time, so a severe winter meant few clams or oysters, mussels or scallops. The settlers therefore "invented" corn oysters.

Corn oysters actually had nothing at all to do with fish.

They were really a type of corn fritter. And yet, when a spoonful of the flour-and-egg batter, chock full of corn kernels, was dropped into the sizzling fat of a hot skillet, the edges of the tiny uneven pancake curled so prettily that it resembled an oyster being simmered for a thick, milk-rich oyster stew.

Corn oysters were just one more example of the New England imagination at work, especially during those thin times when meals had to be built around dried corn, dried beans, and dried fish—all dull, stodgy foods that cried out for variation and disguise. Although they were a far cry from the plump, delicate, fresh oysters the colonists were thinking of, corn oysters were nevertheless very tasty and quite nutritious. In colonial times they were usually eaten liberally doused with maple syrup or honey. They are still good that way. They are also good in modern meals served as a side dish with roast chicken or braised beef and lots of gravy.

Here is the recipe for old-fashioned-type New England corn oysters.

✳ CORN OYSTERS

    2 eggs
   12 level tablespoons flour
  ½ teaspoon salt
  ⅛ teaspoon white pepper
    1 12-ounce can vacuum-packed, whole-kernel corn
       butter or margarine, and oil, for frying

- In a medium-size mixing bowl, beat the two eggs with a

wire whisk. Add the flour, a few tablespoons at a time, and beat smooth. Add salt and pepper, and the corn. There should be about 2 to 3 tablespoons of liquid in the can of corn. Add up to 3 tablespoons, but no more.

• In a deep 10-inch frying pan melt approximately 1 tablespoon of butter or margarine. Add enough oil to cover the surface ¼ inch deep with fat. When fat is hot, drop corn oyster mixture into it from a large tablespoon, forming oval cakes about 3 inches long and 2½ inches wide. When golden-brown on bottom, turn and fry other side.

• Place fried corn oysters on paper toweling to absorb excess fat, and keep in a warm place. Fry in two or three batches until all batter is used up. Serve hot. Makes 18 corn oysters.

Red Flannel Hash
Last Night's Boiled Dinner

✳ Although corn in its various guises supplied breads and stews, porridges and puddings, even "fish," it somehow took meat and vegetables to form the basis for a really hearty and proper meal. But for the New England housewife, often servantless and plagued with dozens of daily chores connected with keeping her family well and her household comfortable, "fancy" cooking was almost completely out of the question. Setting a lavish table was a role better left to the mistresses of the southern plantation houses, which had separate kitchen buildings staffed by five or six black slaves.

Turning out platters of fried chicken and beaten biscuit, numerous side dishes, and elegant desserts, was relatively simple in the mansions of the South when many hands made light work. But in New England, even among the more prosperous families, no-nonsense cooking was the order of the day. And the perfect meal-in-a-pot was the boiled dinner.

It combined meat, potatoes, and other vegetables, all

cooked together in a large kettle suspended from a lug pole that spanned the entire width of the fireplace. The fireplace in the New England colonial home supplied much more than cooking heat, of course. It gave out warmth and light, and was the social and work center around which the entire family clustered.

The great advantage of the fireplace dinner, bubbling away all day in its pot, was that it needed almost no watching. The contents might include chicken or salted codfish, ham or corned beef, along with potatoes and such hardy vegetables as carrots and turnips, onions and parsnips, cabbage and rutabagas. Beets were popular, too, in the boiled dinner but were always cooked separately because they tended to stain everything else in the pot a deep, shocking pink.

After cattle became plentiful enough in the new settlements so that the colonists could afford to slaughter some for food and still keep enough on hand for dairying and farm work, corned beef became the most popular meat to go into the boiled dinner.

Fresh beef was well-liked, too, but the thrifty New Englanders had to think of a way of keeping the valuable meat of a slaughtered beef animal for a fairly long period of time. The best known method of preserving a large cut of beef was by the salting-and-pickling method known as "corning."

For once, this word had nothing at all to do with corn. It really referred to the dried pepper berries, or peppercorns, that helped to spice the meat as it sat in its barrel or tub of pickling brine. Corning beef not only preserved it for months, but it gave it a pleasingly tangy flavor and also broke down the fibers, making it much more tender than

fresh beef. This was especially true if the meat was from an older working animal, as was so often the case, one that had seen its days of drawing a plow across the fields.

The boiled corned beef dinner became so popular in New England that some families had it as often as twice a week. Usually the cooking pot was brought directly from the fireplace to the rough board dining table. The family dipped its only eating implements, large carved wooden spoons, directly into the pot and each member ladled his or her portion into a wooden trencher, a shallow bowl made by hollowing out the top of a round or rectangular block of wood. Poorer families had no trenchers at all. Instead they had hollows carved out of the wooden tabletop itself. These served as places to deposit one's portion of meat, vegetables, and pot liquor.

Puritan families, in particular, had strict rules governing the family's conduct at mealtimes. The father sat at the head of the table flanked by the older boys. The mother, an older daughter, or a hired serving girl took care of their needs at table. The younger children were not even permitted to sit at mealtime. They stood near the foot of the table, observing a respectful silence, and ate whatever was given to them.

Fortunately most of the early colonial dishes, such as soups, stews, porridges, puddings, and even the boiled dinner, could be eaten quite conveniently with a crudely fashioned spoon. But it was common practice to use the fingers freely, too, so the family was provided with large linen napkins that the women of the house spun and wove from home-grown flax.

As time went on, tableware of pewter, earthenware, and even china and silver began to appear on colonial tables.

Two-tined forks came into use around 1700. They were used mainly to anchor a chunk of meat while slicing away at it with one's all-purpose pocket knife. It was not until the middle of the eighteenth century that colonial families began to use table knives for cutting their food into bite-size pieces and three-tined forks for conveying it to their mouths.

As tasty and filling as boiled dinners were, a fairly steady diet of them over a long winter tended to get monotonous. So, instead of serving the reheated leftovers straight from the pot night after night, someone got the good idea to chop up the meat and vegetables and fry them all together in salt-pork drippings or bacon fat, making a thick, crusty-bottomed hash. The brown-edged, omelet-like hash not only tasted a lot different from the soft, soupy boiled dinner, it looked a lot different, too.

One reason was that the leftover beets were chopped and cooked right in with the corned beef and the rest of the vegetables so that the hash was a lovely old-rose color, almost the same soft shade as a piece of slightly faded red flannel. What could be more appropriate than to call the chopped-and-fried leftovers of the New England boiled dinner "red flannel hash!"

Here is a recipe for red flannel hash. Using canned corned beef, canned beets, and boiled potatoes, it can be prepared quite simply, bypassing the step of cooking the boiled dinner itself.

✳ RED FLANNEL HASH

½ cup diced salt pork or diced thick-sliced bacon,
    in ¼-inch squares

 1 12-ounce can corned beef, cut or chopped into ¼-inch
    cubes
 2 cups coarsely chopped cooked beets (use 1 one-pound
    can sliced beets, well-drained)
2½ cups coarsely chopped boiled potatoes
 2 tablespoons dried minced onion
 1 tablespoon dried minced parsley
 ¼ cup milk
    salt and pepper to taste
1½ tablespoons butter or margarine

• Place salt pork or bacon in a deep, heavy-bottomed 10-inch frying pan that has a sloping rim. Fry crisp and brown. Remove salt pork or bacon cracklings with a slotted spoon and set aside. Pour off fat from pan and save.

• In a large mixing bowl, combine the corned beef, beets, potatoes, onion, parsley, milk, and salt and pepper to taste. Return 1 tablespoon of the fat from the salt pork or bacon to the frying pan. Add the 1½ tablespoons of butter or margarine and heat to sizzling.

• Add the hash mixture, pressing it down firmly and evenly in the pan. Reduce heat to low and fry, without stirring or turning, for 45 minutes. Edges and underside should be crisp and brown. Loosen them slightly with a flexible spatula.

• Place a large platter upside down over frying pan. Carefully invert pan and platter so that hash is turned out onto platter like a very large pancake, browned side up. Sprinkle cracklings on top of red flannel hash and serve at once. Serves 5–6.

Apple Pandowdy
Fruits of the First Orchards

✳ Fruits of many kinds grew with wild abandonment all over New England. Vines thickly clustered with grapes, in the Cape Cod area, are said to have inspired the Norsemen of the 11th century to call that region Vinland. And the Pilgrims, soon after their arrival, discovered bushes of purple beach plums along the sandy New England seashore and masses of ruby-toned cranberries in the marshes and boglands. The Pilgrims originally named this fruit "crane berry" because the stem and white blossom of the plant resembled the neck and head of a crane; others have called it the "marsh ruby."

Inland, the New England countryside was dotted with thickets of wild blackberries and huckleberries, gooseberries, strawberries, and raspberries, while wild crabapple trees were to be found almost everywhere. There was only one trouble with this bounty of uncultivated fruit. It was almost all sour, ranging from moderately mouth-puckering to stingingly tart.

The colonists were accustomed to the milder-flavored fruits of Britain, particularly the orchard-grown apples, sometimes eaten out of hand but used mainly in all sorts of tarts and "pyes," puddings and "puffs," fritters and "fools." Sweeteners, of course, had to be added to these English cooked-fruit concoctions, but the acid-tasting fruits of the New World required much more sweetening. And sugar, which had greater sweetening power than either West Indian molasses or New England's honey or maple syrup, was scarce and expensive.

So it is not surprising that as early as 1629, John Winthrop, the governor of the Massachusetts Bay Colony, had English apple trees planted in the Salem area, and by 1634 young apple and pear orchards had been established in many parts of colonial Massachusetts. New England's soil and climate were apparently so well suited to apple-growing that, by the middle of the 18th century, its shining rosy-green fruits were turning up in London fruit stalls and were also in great demand in the West Indies where they were enjoyed by the wealthy white planters and their families. New England's apples also traveled westward across North America through the good offices of that barefoot and tattered tree-planting visionary, Johnny Appleseed, who was actually born John Chapman in Boston around 1775.

The New England settlers devised a number of desserts made with apples and also with huckleberries which, in their cultivated form, were sometimes called blueberries. Most of these desserts were prepared in true New England fireplace-cookery tradition by steaming. The sweetened fruit would be turned into a deep pot, topped with a dough mixture, tightly covered as for a steamed pudding, and suspended over the fire until the fruit was cooked tender and syrupy, and the topping was moistly cakelike or dumplinglike. The dish was always served warm, usually with thick cream poured generously over the top.

Nobody seemed to know what to call these delectable, filling desserts, but pretty soon people began to talk about "apple slump" and "blueberry grunt." The names somehow fit. A slump was heavy and just seemed to collapse out of sheer weariness when it was dished out of the cooking pot onto a plate, especially if the steamed topping hit the plate first and was smothered with the thick fruit mixture and the cream. A grunt, which was really exactly the same thing as a slump, might have earned its name from the grunts of satisfaction of those who spooned down its melting goodness. Or could the name have had something to do with those grunts of digestive distress and discomfort due to overindulgence following a heavy meal?

If slumps and grunts began to get the colonial diner down, there was always flummery, a much more sensible dessert since it consisted only of fruit, sweetening, and a little water, stewed tender and thickened slightly, and served warm with a little cream or custard, no doughy topping. If desired, one *could* layer the fruit mixture with slices of buttered bread. In any case, a dessert known as blackberry flummery came to be very well liked at colonial dinner tables.

Sometimes the fireplace oven was used to bake a deep-dish pie called apple pandowdy. The authentic pandowdy of colonial New England was homely, even ugly in appearance but exquisite in taste. "Dowdy" in those days seemed to have another meaning besides plain or old-fashioned; it meant "to chop." The New England housewife would bake her apple dessert just until the crust was turning crisp and golden. Then she would take it out of the oven and "dowdy" or chop the crust and the apples together into large pieces right in the baking dish or "pan," bake it a little longer, drizzle it with molasses, and serve it up warm with thick, sweet cream.

While most pandowdy and other early apple-pie recipes were sweetened with molasses, Vermont and New Hampshire people made their apple pies with maple syrup, which was extracted from the native sugar-maple trees. Later on, when sugar became more plentiful, the New Englanders began to use cranberries in pies and other desserts. Massachusetts cranberries and imported Spanish raisins were sometimes combined for a "mock cherry pie." Fruit pies, in fact, became so popular as oven-baking facilities improved that by the time the American Revolution was over New Englanders were eating pie for breakfast, a custom that continued right on through the 19th century, which was an era of hearty eating. Apple remained the all-time favorite filling, and the favorite pie apple appeared to be the Rhode Island Greening, a variety grown in and around Newport as early as 1700.

Greenings are fine for the apple pandowdy recipe that follows, and so are other crisp, juicy varieties such as McIntoshes, Cortlands, or Winesaps.

❋ APPLE PANDOWDY

*Pastry**
  1 cup sifted flour
  ½ teaspoon salt

* If preferred, use a commercial pie-crust mix and, following directions on package, make up the amount of pastry for one 9-inch pie shell. Pat pastry dough into a small square and proceed as directed in recipe.

2½ tablespoons lard or vegetable shortening
 3 tablespoons chilled butter
 3 tablespoons cold water

Filling
 6 cups thinly sliced apples (about 8 large apples, washed,
     quartered, cored, and pared)
 ⅓ cup sugar
 ½ teaspoon ground cinnamon
 ⅛ teaspoon ground nutmeg
 ⅛ teaspoon ground cloves
 ⅛ teaspoon salt
 ⅓ cup molasses
   water
 2 tablespoons melted butter
 3 tablespoons molasses

• To prepare pastry, add salt to sifted and measured flour in a mixing bowl. With a pastry blender, or two sharp knives worked in a crisscross motion, cut in the lard or vegetable shortening and the butter until flour-and-shortening mixture resembles coarse bread crumbs. Add the water, one tablespoon at a time, stirring mixture lightly with a fork so that moisture is evenly distributed. Now mix vigorously with fork until dough forms large clumps. Work with fingers into a ball of dough. Flatten ball slightly and shape into a small square.

• Set oven to heat to 425 degrees Fahrenheit.

• Cut off two-thirds of the square of pastry dough. Wrap remaining one-third in wax paper and set aside. Using a floured rolling pin and a floured board or pastry cloth, roll the two-thirds of the pastry dough into a long strip, about 3 inches wide and 21 inches long, and about ⅛-inch thick. Arrange strip to fit around inside wall of a deep 1½-quart casserole or other baking dish. (Do not cover bottom of dish with pastry; only the sides are to be lined). Pastry should stand about ¼-inch higher than rim of casserole. Where ends of strip meet, seal together firmly and press against side of dish.

• Combine apples, sugar, cinnamon, nutmeg, cloves, and salt. Measure the ⅓-cup molasses and add enough water to make ½ cup. Blend, and add this mixture and melted butter to apples.

• Roll out remaining one-third of pastry dough into a circle just slightly larger than the top of the casserole dish. Turn apple mixture into casserole. Place circle of pastry on top and tuck edges in all around inside rim of dish, overlapping standing rim of pastry.

• Bake pandowdy at 425 degrees for 25 minutes, or until crust is pale golden-brown. Remove pandowdy from oven and reset oven heat to 350 degrees. With two sharp knives, "dowdy" all of the crust and apples by cutting them at a crisscross into pieces of about ¾ to 1 inch, allowing some of the syrupy mixture from underneath to bubble up. Do not, however, chop crust and apples too fine or mash them.

• Now place a cover on the casserole dish and return it to the oven to bake at 350 degrees for 20 minutes longer. Remove dish from oven, take off cover, drizzle pandowdy with the 3 tablespoons of molasses, and bake, uncovered, for 10 minutes more. Serve apple pandowdy warm, directly from baking dish. Makes 6 to 8 servings.

The Middle Atlantic Colonies

Breadbasket of the New World

When Henry Hudson first sailed the *Half Moon* up the placid river that was later to take his name, the shores quickly came alive with Indians who aimed their canoes, laden with furs and tobacco, toward the Dutch ship. The year was 1609, and the English captain who represented the Dutch East India Company was delighted to offer penknives and bead trinkets, strips of brightly colored cloth, and drafts of Holland gin in exchange for the rich, warm pelts of beaver and otter, and for the strange green leaves of the Americas that were becoming so popular to smoke in Europe.

Following Hudson's voyage, the Dutch set up permanent fur-trading posts along the river, and years went by with no one dreaming of the untapped agricultural wealth of the region. The Indians of this Middle Atlantic territory, both Algonquians and Iroquois, raised the usual crops of corn, squash, pumpkins, and beans. They dug and caught shellfish from the shores of Long Island and Chesapeake Bay, took shad from the Hudson and snapping turtles from the fresh-water ponds, captured wild game, waterfowl, and passenger pigeons, and were very fond of fat dogs, which they raised specifically for the cooking pot.

It was not until after the arrival of the first Dutch settlers, on the ship *Nieuw Nederlandt* in 1623, that the real secrets of the soil began to be unlocked. The Dutch settled on Long Island and on Manhattan Island, on both shores of the Hudson, and upriver at what is now Albany. Unlike the early New England settlers, they came to the New World by choice rather than necessity. Through an arrangement with the newly formed Dutch West India Company, they were able to obtain land, with trading and farming privileges, which became theirs if they remained on it for six years. Livestock, farm implements, seed, and other supplies were brought over in abundance, and pretty soon the Dutch were planting wheat, barley, rye, and buckwheat in the Hudson Valley and elsewhere with remarkable success. The land was less rocky and more sweeping than that of New England, and the soil and climate appeared ideally suited to European grains. If this had not been the case, it is possible that the Dutch, who were great lovers of all sorts of breadstuffs, would not have stayed on, preferring to return to the comfortable life they had known in Holland.

As it was, the New Netherland estate-owners proceeded to cultivate the land lavishly, to recreate the bustling blue-tiled kitchens of their home country, and to set hearty and even sumptuous tables, often attended by friends and always by good cheer. Washington Irving, that chronicler of early Dutch days in and around Tarrytown, New York, where he made his home from 1835 until his death in 1859, describes the lands of the prosperous Dutch gentleman farmers, in *The Legend of Sleepy Hollow.*

As Ichabod Crane, the lovesick schoolmaster, approaches the "mansion" house of the comfortable Van Tassel family, he surveys with delight the "great fields of Indian corn . . . holding out the promise of cakes and hasty-pudding; and the yellow pumpkins . . . giving ample prospects of the most luxurious of pies." Apples hung "in oppressive opulence on the trees; some gathered into baskets and barrels for the market; others heaped up in rich piles for the cider-press." And best of all, there were the "fragrant buckwheat fields breathing the odor of the bee-hive," at which "soft anticipations stole over his mind of dainty slapjacks, well buttered, and garnished with honey or treacle, by the delicate little dimpled hand of Katrina Van Tassel."

There was indeed plenty of butter and cheese, as well as milk and cream, in the Dutch households, for the settlers had brought herds of dairy cattle and other livestock with them. At the large midday dinner there was often a Holland *hutspot* (or hodgepodge), a slow-cooked dish of corned beef, salt pork, carrots, and turnips, to which the New World Dutch added Indian cornmeal. And other hearty dishes included steaming thick pea soups, roast pork with cabbage, and roast goose with dumplings. In addition to these home-grown foods, the tables of the New Netherland Dutch were also well provided with imports of sugar, spices, dried fruits, tea, chocolate, wines, and brandies, for Holland was one of the world's most prosperous mercantile powers.

For many years fur-trading continued to provide added income, making it possible for many of the new landowners to hire or purchase farm and household labor and so expand

their estates. As early as 1626, the same year that Manhattan Island was purchased from the Indians, Dutch ships began bringing black slaves from West Africa to work on the plantationlike farms on Long Island and at Albany. Soon the wheatfields were producing enough grain to supply New England and the Southern colonies and also to export fine white flour to Holland, along with shipments of tobacco, lumber, and animal pelts. But long after the animals had been hunted out and the fur trade began to diminish, agriculture remained an important commercial mainstay of Dutch colonial life, as well as the source of its basic foodstuff, wheat flour. And even after the English took over in 1664 and the colony of New Netherland became New York, the cultivation of wheat and other cereal grains continued to flourish so steadily that New York, in the late 1700s, became the "granary of the Revolution."

This first breadbasket of the New World extended into other parts of the Middle Atlantic region: across the Hudson into New Jersey and Delaware, which were settled by both the Swedish and the Dutch, and especially into Pennsylvania. Beginning in 1682, Pennsylvania became a refuge for the much-persecuted Society of Friends (originating in England and popularly known as Quakers), as well as for several austere and hardworking German religious sects.

The immigrant Germans, who were dubbed the "Pennsylvania Dutch" by their English Quaker neighbors (because the word *Deutsch* sounded closer to "Dutch" than to "German") fanned out from Philadelphia into the tranquil farm country of southeastern Pennsylvania and established a unique way of life that has hardly changed at all since 1700. Many of the "plain people"—Amish, Mennonite, Dunkard

—have clung to the simple existence dictated by their religion, wearing unadorned homemade clothing, traveling by horse and buggy, and rejecting modern conveniences like telephones, plumbing, and electricity. Frugality has always been a keynote, and yet their generosity with food is summed up in such popular local sayings as "Eat yourself full," and "Come in and shovel yourself out."

The food traditions of these German settlers included noodles and dumplings, pretzels and coffee cakes, breads, rolls, and pies, so it was necessary to plant wheat and to mill flour. Like the Dutch in New Netherland, they were lucky in being able to reproduce many of the dishes of their homeland. Of course, they also grew maize and using this food they created new recipes like scrapple, which combined German pork-sausage ingredients with Indian cornmeal. Scrapple was made at hog-slaughtering time because it was a good way to use up the pork scraps and trimmings. After the meat mixture was extended with the addition of the cornmeal mush, it was molded in oblong forms and would then be sliced and fried crisp for a hearty breakfast along with eggs and fried apples.

Thinking ahead to the long winter, the Pennsylvania Dutch preserved all sorts of harvest foods. They dehydrated the tender summer-ripe kernels of sweet corn by sun-drying or oven-drying, later using them in soups and stews. They also preserved the apples and pears from their orchards by slicing them into wedge-shaped pieces and drying them. The dried fruit slices were called *Schnitz* from the word meaning "slice" or "cut." One of the most famous of all Pennsylvania Dutch dishes was called *Schnitz un Knepp*, cooked dried apples or pears and large feathery dumplings, with a chunk of ham tossed into the pot or, among poorer families, a ham bone for flavor.

Even in the most modest farm households, a proper meal had to have its accompaniments of "seven sweets and seven sours." This was almost a superstition among the Pennsylvania Dutch, as necessary for warding off evil spirits and acts of witchery as the hex signs that decorated their barns to keep the milch cows from going dry. The sweets and sours were relishes, each prepared in the proper season from farm-grown products and put away for long-keeping in jars and crocks, barrels and kegs. There were pickled watermelon rind and spiced seckel pears, apple butter and lemon honey, jams, jellies, and marmalades for the sweets; corn, pepper, and green tomato relish, sweet, dill, and sour pickles, pickled eggs, pickled beets, and all sorts of marinated vegetables for the sours.

It was said of the Pennsylvania Dutch that even when food was at its scarcest they could produce marvelous, tasty, hot, filling dishes. One such recipe was called stone soup. It went something like this: take a large, smooth, round stone from the fields and scrub it very, very well; place it in a large pot and fill with water; add carrots, onions, turnips, potatoes, and pepper and salt; cook until done and serve steaming hot!

Just as New England's corn and cornmeal traveled westward with the passage of time and the opening up of new frontiers, so the wheat-growing of the Middle Atlantic region crossed the mountains of Pennsylvania and headed for the prairies and the plains. In some of the new regions like the Blue Ridge and Kentucky, wheat did not do well and corn had to be planted. In other places, the sites of present-day Kansas, North Dakota, Washington, Montana, and Nebraska, wheat began to be produced in large quantities. Today these states, in the order given, are the leading growers, making up the modern breadbasket of the U.S.A.

While most of the New England states have nowadays dropped the cultivation of basic agricultural crops on a major scale (with the exception of potatoes in Maine and tobacco in Connecticut and Massachusetts), Pennsylvania is still a wheat-growing state. Of course, its ten million bushels produced annually are a far cry from the well over 300 million bushels grown in Kansas. And New York's five million bushels are indeed modest. But it is warming to know that, if the original breadbasket of the New World has been transplanted to the vast tracts of the Midwest, the Great Plains, and the Far West, at least a few tasty crumbs can still be credited to the pioneering wheat farmers of the Middle Atlantic region.

Snickerdoodles
Dutch Treats

✳ The Dutch colonists of New Netherland were so fond of "bakers' meats"—cakes and cookies, hotbreads and quickbreads, and all sorts of other wheaten specialties—that they took the trouble to bring their long-handled waffle-irons with them from Holland. Waffles, from the Dutch word *wafel* (weave), were an Old World favorite made by pouring a batter into a pair of sizzling-hot irons. Once the hinged irons were clamped together, the batter baked quickly into a tasty hot cake. The woven design of bumps and partitions on the inside surfaces of the irons insured rapid, even baking.

Cookies, baked in similar fashion in wafer-irons, were called *izer koekjes* (iron cookies). The wafer-irons were impressed with designs and sometimes with the owner's initials, which then appeared on the baked cookie. *Doed koeks* (funeral cakes) were thick round cookies made with caraway seed that were identified with the initials of the deceased. They were passed out at funerals and were often not eaten at all, but taken home by the mourners and kept for years as mementos of the dead.

When the New World Dutch were not baking sweet cakes in heated iron molds, they were frying them in deep pots of boiling lard. The *oliekoek* or *olykoek* (oil cake) was the ancestor of the doughnut as we know it today. It was round and puffy and coated with sugar, sometimes with a few raisins or some chopped sweetened apple tucked inside it. The idea of the hole in the doughnut came a little later on. The removal of the "nut" of dough from the middle did away with the sometimes soggy inside of the *olykoek* and offered more crisp eating edges.

But let Ichabod Crane (or rather Washington Irving) tell about it, as our hero entered the parlor of the Van Tassel mansion and beheld "the ample charms of a genuine Dutch country tea-table in the sumptuous time of autumn. Such heaped-up platters of cakes of various and almost indescribable kinds, known only to experienced Dutch housewives! There was the doughty dough-nut, the tenderer oly koek, and the crisp and crumbling cruller; sweet-cakes and short-cakes, ginger-cakes and honey-cakes, and the whole family of cakes. And then there were apple-pies and peach-pies and pumpkin-pies . . . delectable dishes of preserved plums, and peaches, and pears, and quinces . . . together with bowls of milk and cream . . . with the motherly tea-pot sending up its clouds of vapor from the midst . . ."

There was also a more homely side to Dutch dining in New Netherland, of course. There were the cereals and porridges eaten at breakfast and supper, including an Indian-cornmeal-and-milk porridge called *suppawn;* there were whole-grain loaves of dark, crunchy wheaten bread as

well as the finer white-flour loaves. Country people baked their bread in their fireplace ovens, but in the more sophisticated community of New Amsterdam (as Manhattan Island was called after 1653) there were public bakeries and even a set of laws fixing the prices of baked goods and governing the kinds of breads and cakes to be sold.

No bakery could sell sweet cakes or cookies unless it also had bread for sale, and "coarse" loaves, which usually weighed anywhere from two to eight pounds, had to be offered for sale along with the finer loaves. The colonial authorities of New Netherland even took care to regulate the amount of tobacco that could be grown, so that an adequate proportion of land would be given over to the cultivation of grain and other edible crops.

Homemade cakes and cookies that were neither baked in heated irons nor fried in hot lard or oil could be baked in the fireplace oven along with the family's bread. There were cookies known as puffards, jumbles, and wonders, and one type that went by the delightfully funny name of snickerdoodles.

The story of how this cookie got its name is wreathed in mystery. "Snicker" may have come from the Dutch word *snekrad,* which means snail-wheel and applies to one of the round wheels found in clockworks; on the other hand, "snicker" may have come from the German *Schnecke,* meaning snail. The Germans also give the name *Schnecke* to a sweet bun made of cinnamon-sprinkled dough, rolled up pinwheel-fashion and sliced to resemble snails. Snickerdoodles are not nearly so fancy or complicated, but they do have cinnamon and sugar sprinkled on their tops.

Whatever their beginnings, these delicate little cakelike drop cookies soon earned a place at the colonial Dutch tea-table and later turned up in Connecticut, Pennsylvania, and western New York State, where they are still favorites. Here is a recipe for snickerdoodles that is derived from early days in New Netherland and owes its existence to the foresight and bounty of the Dutch wheat farmers and to the industry of their merry, energetic housewives.

❋ SNICKERDOODLES

½ cup butter or margarine (¼ pound or 1 stick)
¾ cup sugar
1 egg
2 cups flour
1½ teaspoons baking powder
½ teaspoon salt
½ cup milk
½ teaspoon vanilla extract
2 tablespoons sugar
2 teaspoons cinnamon

• Set oven to heat to 325 degrees Fahrenheit.

• Put butter or margarine in large mixing bowl and allow it to soften at room temperature. Press with the back of a wooden mixing spoon until creamy and smooth. Add sugar gradually and continue creaming until well blended. Add egg and beat well.

• Sift flour into a separate bowl. Measure off 2 cups, add baking powder and salt, and sift again. Combine milk and vanilla extract. Add one-third of flour mixture to butter-sugar-and-egg mixture. Blend smooth. Add half the milk mixture and combine thoroughly. Add next third of flour mixture and blend; add second half of milk and mix well. Finally, add last third of flour mixture and mix dough to smooth consistency.

• In a small bowl combine the 2 tablespoons sugar and 2 teaspoons of cinnamon, and set aside. Butter a large cookie sheet, about 12 x 15 inches. Using a spoon and a knife, drop mounds of dough by the heaping teaspoonful onto the cookie sheet, placing them about two inches apart (about 15 cookies to the sheet). Sprinkle each mound of dough generously with the cinnamon-and-sugar mixture.

• Bake cookies in three batches, about 15 minutes each, or until cookies are lightly browned around edges and centers spring back when touched lightly. Remove to cooling racks. When thoroughly cool, store in a tightly covered tin. Makes about 45 snickerdoodles.

Shoo-Fly Pie
More with Molasses

✳ When it came to bake-ovens, the Pennsylvania Dutch forsook the limited fireplace oven, which was little more than a shelf built into the brick or stone fireplace wall, and erected immense outdoor ovens of stone. Their cavelike interiors, six or seven feet wide, were capable of accommodating half a dozen bread loaves, as many pies and crumb cakes, and several batches of cookies all at the same time. As Pennsylvania Dutch families were large, and extra help was usually taken on at harvest time, there was an unending demand for baked goods of all sorts.

Even pretzels, which the Germans introduced to America, were baked on the Pennsylvania Dutch farms until well into the 19th century when the first commercial pretzel bakeries were established in the region. In Europe, pretzels had been the bread of itinerant holy men and other travelers as long ago as the time of the First Crusade in the 11th century. The twisted arms of the pretzel were said to represent the arms of a worshipper crossed in prayer, and the different-sized openings in the pretzel made it easy for religious pilgrims to string them onto their staffs. The Pennsylvania Dutch baked both crisp and soft pretzels and made a nourishing meal out of them by inventing a "pretzel soup" consisting of a bowl of hot milk and melted butter filled with broken-up pretzels.

If the New Netherland Dutch were famous for the cakes, cookies, and crullers at their tea-tables, the Pennsylvania Dutch were renowned for their warm and fragrant kaffee-klatsch offerings. The spacious farmhouse kitchens were centers for the enjoyment of *Streusel Kuchen* (crumb cakes), *Semmeln* (sweet rolls), and *Schnecken* (cinnamon buns) along with coffee and talk, when the busy routine of the household permitted. Back in the German-settled community of Philadelphia, which was known as Germantown, *Schnecken* were gradually transformed into "Philadelphia sticky buns." The little snail-like pinwheels of dough, often with raisins and nuts tucked into them, were baked in muffin cups that had been liberally sprinkled with brown sugar or doused with honey or syrup. After being baked, the buns were turned upside down and the tops and sides glistened with a tantalizingly sticky coating that made licking the fingers very pleasant.

When the large outdoor farmhouse ovens were cooling, in between bakings, they were a good place for slow-drying mountains of cut-up apples for *Schnitz*. Then, later in the autumn and through the winter came the *Schnitz* pies, tasting almost as good as fresh apple. But as the dried fruits of the previous summer began to be used up, the inventive Pennsylvania Dutch housewife had to look around for other ideas for pie fillings, fillings that called for neither fruit nor eggs nor cream, all of which were in low supply at that time of year. The one thing she did have plenty of was flour, and another inexpensive staple was molasses, that dependable by-product of West Indian sugar-cane extraction.

So the Pennsylvania Dutch housewife devised something new. She prepared a flour-butter-and-sugar mixture that resembled the *Streusel* or crumb topping she used on her coffee cakes and combined heavy sprinklings of this with spoonfuls of molasses in a pie shell, letting the dry and the wet ingredients blend of their own accord in the baking. Of course, some of the molasses formed dark, sticky patches on the top, and when the baked pie was set on the window-ledge to cool, it was a favorite stopping place for the flies that hovered near the farmhouse kitchen. Somebody had to keep constant watch lest a few buzzing black flies became pasted to the molasses, so what could be a more appropriate name for this pie than "shoo-fly!"

Actually, there were several types of shoo-fly pie, depending on the proportion of crumb mixture to molasses. The dryer type was almost like a coffee cake set into a pie crust and was often eaten at breakfast time. It was good dunked in hot milk or coffee. The "wet" shoo-fly pie was more of a dessert, since it contained plenty of sweetly oozing molasses.

The following recipe is for a fairly wet Pennsylvania Dutch shoo-fly pie. Although not traditional, this pie is very good topped with gobs of whipped cream or with vanilla or butter pecan ice cream.

✳ SHOO-FLY PIE

*Pie Crust**

- 1 cup sifted flour
- ½ teaspoon salt
- 2½ tablespoons lard or vegetable shortening
- 3 tablespoons chilled butter
- 3 tablespoons cold water

Pie Filling

CRUMB MIXTURE

- 1½ cups sifted flour
- ½ cup brown sugar
- ½ teaspoon ground cinnamon
- ⅛ teaspoon ground nutmeg
- ⅛ teaspoon ground ginger
- ¼ cup butter (4 tablespoons; ½ stick)

MOLASSES MIXTURE

- ¾ cup hot water
- ½ teaspoon baking soda
- ¾ cup molasses

• To prepare pie crust, add salt to sifted and measured flour in a mixing bowl. With a pastry blender, or two sharp knives worked in a crisscross motion, cut in the lard or vegetable shortening and the butter until the flour-and-shortening mixture resembles coarse bread crumbs. Add the water, one tablespoon at a time, stirring mixture lightly with a fork so that moisture is evenly distributed. Now mix

* If preferred, make up pastry (for one 9-inch pie shell) from a commercial pie-crust mix, following directions on package, or use a prepared, unbaked 9-inch pie shell.

vigorously with fork until dough forms large clumps. Work with fingers into a ball of dough, place it on a floured board or pastry cloth, flatten it slightly, and roll with a floured rolling pin into a circle about 11 inches in diameter. Fit pastry loosely into a 9-inch pie plate and, with floured fingers, form a standing rim of dough and pinch or flute as desired.

• Set oven to heat to 425 degrees Fahrenheit. Place pie crust in refrigerator while preparing filling. Combine first five ingredients of crumb mixture, making sure that brown sugar is pressed down firmly to measure. Cut in butter as described for pie crust, but after particles are reduced to size of peas, work mixture with fingertips until shortening is well blended with flour.

• To prepare molasses mixture, add soda to hot water and let it dissolve. Add molasses and mix well. Take pie shell from refrigerator. Sprinkle bottom with a light layer of the crumb mixture. Now add one-third of the molasses mixture, top with one-third of the remaining crumb mixture, and repeat twice.

• Bake pie at 425 degrees for 10 minutes, then reduce oven setting to 350 and bake 20 to 25 minutes longer or until crust is browned and crumb mixture is firm. (Place a large flat pan or a sheet of aluminum foil on oven shelf beneath pie plate in case some of molasses mixture runs over during baking.) Shoo-fly pie is best served warm or at room temperature, and does not need to be stored in refrigerator.

The Southern Colonies

Starvation in a Land of Plenty

Shortly before dawn, on a day in late April of the year 1607, the passengers of three small English vessels had their first glimpse of "the Land of Virginia," which was to become the site of the first permanent English settlement in the New World. Before the day was out, the newcomers—over one hundred men and boys—had their first brush with hostile Indians, an omen of some of the many hardships that lay in wait in the untried North American wilderness.

George Percy, one of the passengers, wrote of this event, "there came the Savages, creeping upon all fours from the Hills, like Beares, with their bowes in their mouthes . . ." After wounding two of the party, the Indians who were probably Powhatans of the Algonquian family, having "spent their arrowes, and felt the sharpnesse of our shot . . . retired in to the woods with a great noise, and so left us . . ."

Ignoring this rather bad start on the new continent (which showed the Europeans' insensitivity to the rights and justifiable reactions of the American Indians), Percy went on to describe the animal and plant life in and around the settlement, some sixty miles upriver from Chesapeake Bay, where the fort of Jamestown was built. "We found store of Turkie nests and many egges. We also did see many squirrels, Conies, Black Birds . . . and divers other fowles . . . This countrey is a fruitfull soile, bearing many goodly and fruitfull trees, as mulberries, cherries, walnuts, ceders, cypresse, sassafras, and vines in great abundance."

The true abundance, however, that the Jamestown adventurers hoped to find was one of precious metals—gold and silver—as had the Spanish explorers and conquerors in Mexico and South America. They had not expected to dig in for a long stretch as Virginia farmers and householders; they had not even brought any women with them. Many of their company were of "gentleman" status, unaccustomed to manual labor; others were roisterers and soldiers of fortune. So little idea did the immigrants have of life in untamed North America that, instead of farmers, laborers, and simple craftsmen, their party included goldsmiths, jewelers, hat-makers, and even a perfume-maker!

In June, six weeks after arrival, the three ships that had landed the Jamestown men sailed for England, and rations fell low as they waited for fresh supplies and for reinforcements of carpenters, toolmakers, and other skilled workmen. From the writings of Captain John Smith and others who remained behind in Virginia, we learn that the men now began to subsist on one or two cups a day of wheat and barley porridge. The grain, however, after more than four months in the ships' holds, "contained as many worms as graines . . ." Fifty, of the 104 who landed, died between May and September, and those who managed to survive "lived upon Sturgeon, and Sea-crabs . . ." Wistfully, Smith and his companions wrote, "our drinke was water, our lodgings Castles in the ayre . . ."

But the worst was yet to come. While Smith went off on scouting missions and to try to deal with the Indians, whose unpredictable attitudes toward the baffling intruders ranged from amicable to warlike, the Jamestowners panned futilely in the streams for gold instead of learning to grow corn and other crops, or even hunt game. They squabbled among themselves and with their leaders and fell ill from the brackish, swampy drinking water. They were rendered helpless by the extremes of heat in summer and frost in winter, so different from the more temperate year-round climate they had known in England. And finally, toward the close of 1607, they saw the whole of Jamestown—fort, wooden cabins, and stockade—go up in flames.

In 1608, the enterprising and commanding Smith officially took over the government of the colony and things were somewhat better, although the men persisted in their habit of buying food from the Indians, instead of growing or catching their own, and paying for these provisions with guns and gunshot. The first women reached Jamestown in 1609, providing wives for the men (who now included many new arrivals) and hopes that the settlement would begin to take root. But in that same year, Smith was seriously wounded in a powder explosion, believed to have been an attempt on his life, and was forced to return to England for medical treatment. He never saw Virginia again.

Now the most awful time in all of Jamestown's brief and terrible history was upon it. Without Smith's leadership and the good will he had promoted between the settlers and the local Indian chief, Powhatan, and his daughter, Pocahontas, Indian cooperation fell off and attacks resumed. Even worse, a seven-months "starving time" now befell the settlers. Between October of 1609 and April of 1610, the James-towners were reduced to eating roots and acorns, snakes and rats. When even these ran out, in the hard frost of winter, they took to gnawing on boiled shoes, and finally, as their numbers dwindled and many became crazed, some resorted to cannibalism. The victims included dead Indians, and there was even the report of a Jamestown man who consumed portions of his dead wife after pickling her in brine, a crime for which he was later executed.

By late spring of 1610, only about one-tenth of the 600 men and women who had witnessed the turning of the leaves the previous autumn were still alive. Jamestown seemed well on its way to extinction, sharing a fate similar to that of the Lost Colony. The latter settlement, established by Sir Walter Raleigh in 1585 on Roanoke Island, off the coast of North Carolina, had vanished without a trace by 1590. Only the timely arrival, in June of 1610, of a supply expedition from England under the command of Baron de la Warr saved the Jamestown settlement and insured the British colonization of Virginia.

How amazed a southern Rip Van Winkle would have been if he could have fallen asleep at Jamestown in the year 1610 to awaken twenty years later on the very same bank of the James River! Instead of the wilderness surrounding the rough wooden stockade, within which crude dwelling hovels nestled, he would have seen neat clearings and broad fields planted with a green, leafy crop. This was not the "sotweed" of the Virginia Indians but a high-quality West Indian tobacco, seed of which had first been introduced into the Virginia soil by one of the colonists, John Rolfe, in 1612. He would have seen black men working in these fields, Africans that had been brought to the New World as slaves, the first of them arriving at Jamestown as cargo on a Dutch ship in 1619.

Upon inquiry among the townspeople, he would have learned that peaceful relations with the Indians now existed, based on events such as the marriage of John Rolfe to Pocahontas. He would also have heard that Smith had recovered from his wounds and, in 1614, returned to the New World to explore and name New England, and to map the area for the Pilgrims who had landed there successfully in 1620.

It is interesting to note that, despite the hideous lessons of the "starving time" of 1609–10, the Jamestown settlers seemed bent on concentrating on schemes for extracting instant wealth from the Virginia colony rather than on the growing of food. After it became evident that there was not a single grain of gold or vein of silver to be found anywhere in the region, the would-be entrepreneurs, admittedly with encouragement from the British land company and the crown, tried their skills at glass-blowing, wine-making, silk culture, and even lumbering. None amounted to anything until Rolfe thought of tobacco cultivation.

The European demand for tobacco had been growing since Columbus's day. By the early 1600s, smoking it was not only a pleasurable pastime and a social ceremony in Europe but was considered to be therapeutic, a means of destroying harmful germs both within the body and without, and a remedy for a variety of ailments and weaknesses. If, in actuality, tobacco smoke had none of these medicinal advantages and was, in fact, quite opposite

in its effects on the human body, nobody knew it at the time. One thing tobacco did do very effectively—and which no one could contest—was to obliterate the evil and sickening odors that hung ever in the air in closely occupied or thickly populated living quarters before the days of modern plumbing and other sanitary developments.

So, if Indian corn was the life-giving mainstay of colonial New England, and wheat was both the food staple and the source of prosperity for the Middle Atlantic colonies, tobacco was the fortune of the South. Much more than hasty pudding on the table or tea cakes in the oven, tobacco was a valuable medium of exchange. It was the gateway to the immense riches that bought high-ceilinged mansions, vast tracts of cultivated lands, innumerable black house servants and field laborers, and a gracious and elegant style of living that rivaled or outdid that of the landed gentry back home in Britain.

Of course, great wealth did not come to everybody in the Southern colonies. There were the slaves, at the opposite end of the social and economic scale from the plantation-owning families. In between, there were the modest farmers, tradesmen, and craftsmen; the poor who had to work as indentured servants for years to pay off the cost of their passage to the New World; and the destitute dregs of the free white society, who adapted as best they could to half-savage lives in the wilderness. From time to time, Virginia received contingents of jailbirds, homeless women, and orphaned children, sent out from Britain as a means of relieving social problems at home and repopulating or expanding the colony. Many migrated from Virginia to become poor dirt farmers in North Carolina, while the

Georgia colony, established in 1733, began as a refuge for debtors who had been released from prison.

Proof, however, that the coastal region of the Southern colonies was of "a fruitfull soile," as George Percy had observed, and that the Jamestown settlers had indeed starved in a land of plenty through a mixture of laziness, ignorance, indifference, and a measure of bad luck, was clearly shown by the experience of the Maryland settlers who landed in 1634.

Led by English Catholic aristocrats who wanted to avoid religious persecution in Britain, this group of about three hundred Catholic and Protestant farmers and laborers went to work at once raising corn, beans, squash, and peas, and growing orchards of apple and apricot trees. They brought hogs, cows, and chickens with them and obtained turkeys and partridges, crabs and oysters from the Indians, who were both friendly and helpful. It was reported that the Maryland bean vines sprang up out of the rich soil so rapidly that one could watch them climb and that the trees bore so much fruit that some of it had to be fed to the hogs.

At least the Jamestown experience was of value to those who followed in settlements all up and down the eastern seaboard of North America. And the wealth and leisure that Virginia's tobacco cultivation produced gave the new land many distinguished men as well as historic centers of colonial government such as Williamsburg, Virginia. Both played a key role in the movement toward independence that culminated in the American Revolution.

Hush Puppies
Fishfry Food

✳ "Surely there is no place in the world where the inhabitants live with less labor than in North Carolina. Indian corn is of so great increase that a little pains will subsist a very large family with bread."

So wrote William Byrd II, a wealthy Virginia planter, the heir to one of the largest tobacco estates in the colony and the master of another. In 1728, Byrd was part of a commission of leading Virginians who were appointed to survey the dividing line that was to become the boundary between Virginia and North Carolina. The party crossed the Great Dismal Swamp, following the trail of the earlier Virginia settlers who had first migrated south in the 1650s.

The North Carolina farms were in no way comparable to the Virginia plantations. But, as Byrd observed, the corn grew easily, the cattle and hogs foraged for themselves in the swamps and marshes, the women did most of the work, and the men appeared to "loiter away their lives . . ." Perhaps Byrd, the cultivated and busy man of affairs, glanced with passing envy at the simple Carolina dirt farmer who could lean absently on his hoe for hours and even take the time to go fishing without giving a thought to responsibilities left behind him.

In any case, corn did ably supply the basic daily rations of the Carolina families. It appeared in various forms, often as one kind or another of Southern hotbread such as hoecake, ashcake, corn pone, or corn dodger. In the warmer southern climate, cooking was more often done out of doors than in New England. Quickbreads could be baked in the fields, on hunting or fishing expeditions, or simply in front of the farm-cabin doorway.

Hoecake and ashcake were made of cornmeal and salt, water or milk, and usually pork dripping—the fat that fried out or was skimmed off when pork was cooked. The dough had to be stiff enough to be molded into a small, flat cake. Hoecake was so named because the cake of dough was placed on the blade of the farmer's hoe (scrubbed clean, one hopes), which was then set over an open fire in the corn or tobacco field. The long-handled farm hoe served as both baking pan and baker's shovel, conveniently providing a hot, fresh bread for the outdoor noonday meal.

Ashcake or ashbread was quite the same thing except that it was placed directly in the hot ashes of the fire, either outdoors or in the cabin fireplace. To keep the gritty ash from coating the bread, it was customary, in the South, to wrap the dough in a cabbage leaf. The corn pone of the South was a little different from that of New England. It was usually shaped as an irregular lump and then boiled like a dumpling in "pot likker," the flavorsome broth from the simmering of ham and greens.

When corn pone was baked in the oven, the dough was

usually dropped by spoonfuls onto a baking sheet and the resulting knobs of bread were called corn dodger because they were generally so hard it was advisable to dodge if one was thrown in your direction! Of course, there was also the richer and more delicate cornbread made from a batter that was poured into the pan, cut into squares as soon as it was baked, and served hot, slathered with butter. But for the most part, the poorer Southern farm households kept to the more primitive Indian forms of cornbread much longer than did the New England settlers.

"The only business here is the raising of hogs," Byrd wrote of the people of the North Carolina frontier, "which is managed with the least trouble, and affords the diet they are most fond of." While pork, salted or fresh, probably found its way into the family cooking pot more often than any other domesticated meat, the settlers also had easy access to the North Carolina coast, with its bays and inlets and sounds, and also to numerous rivers that flowed eastward to the Atlantic. Clams, crabs, and oysters were plentiful near the shore, frogs and turtles frequented the bayous and ponds, and the rivers were jumping with catfish and bream, bass and trout.

Fishing and hunting trips were especially popular with groups of men and boys, who would make overnight camp near a running stream and sit around the fire long past dark, frying the sweet-fleshed, fresh-caught fish and telling vivid tales of both real and imagined exploits. A sack of cornmeal, either the white or the yellow variety, was always taken along on such expeditions. It was used both to coat the fish, which was then fried in hot lard in an iron skillet over the fire, and to make little balls of corn-pone mixture, which were fried in the fat right along with the fish.

As the hot, crusty balls browned along with the frying fish, the latter gave off such a delicious odor that the hunting dogs that always accompanied their masters began to whine with unbearable longing. To quiet the pleading hounds, the fishermen or huntsmen would toss them some of the savory fried cornmeal pones with the words, "Hush, puppy!" And so the famous hush puppies of the American South received their name. They are popular to this day as fishfry food, served along with a Georgia or Mississippi catfish dinner or with a fried seafood platter from the Carolina banks.

The following hush puppy recipe is a slightly richer, improved Southern version of the early fishing-camp variety. While traditional with fried fish, there is no reason why hush puppies cannot be enjoyed with fried chicken or with braised or roasted meats.

✳ HUSH PUPPIES

1 cup white cornmeal
1 teaspoon baking powder
1 teaspoon salt
⅛ teaspoon white pepper
½ teaspoon sugar
¼ cup milk
¼ cup water
1 egg, beaten
2 tablespoons finely cut onion (optional)
  vegetable oil or lard for frying

• In a bowl, combine the cornmeal, baking powder, salt, pepper, and sugar. Mix together the milk, water, and beaten

egg. Add to the dry ingredients and blend smooth. Add the onion.

• Into a deep, heavy skillet, pour vegetable oil to a depth of ¼ inch, or add enough lard to melt to a similar amount of fat. When fat is hot, drop mounds of hush-puppy mixture into it by the rounded teaspoonful. Each mound should be about the size of a large walnut. Fry until golden-brown on bottom, turn, and fry other side. Remove with a slotted spoon and drain on absorbent paper. When all the hush puppies have been fried, serve at once. Hush puppies may be kept warm for a short while in a 200-degree oven. Makes about 18 hush puppies.

Spoon Bread
Finger Lickin' Porridge

✳ In the great houses of Virginia, such as the James River tobacco plantations, cornbreads were eaten regularly in the slave cabins but came to the master's table much less often. Wheat, which did not do especially well in the South, was shipped from the Middle Atlantic region, and fine, delicate breads made with white flour were baked several times a day by the slave women of the kitchen staff and brought to the table fresh from the oven for each meal.

In addition to their separate kitchen buildings, which kept heat, smoke, and cooking odors away from the great house, the Virginia plantations had a bevy of other outbuildings. These included a smokehouse, where the hams were hung for curing, and a dairy house, which was generally built right over a bubbling spring so that the crocks of cream, butter, and milk could be immersed in the chilly water for longer keeping. Some estates even boasted an ice-house where blocks of winter-cut pond ice could be stored in a cave or dugout for use in summer refreshments such as mint juleps, ice cream, and other frozen desserts.

There was also a laundry building, a carpentry shop, a carriage house, stables, and blacksmith shop, and of course the cabins in which the slave families lived. Each plantation was, in fact, a small village unto itself, providing for almost all its needs. A plantation often possessed its own wharf and warehouse where the landowners could take direct delivery of goods ordered from New England, the West Indies, or Europe. Aside from the larger towns like Virginia's Williamsburg, Maryland's Annapolis, and South Carolina's Charleston, which were the law-making, social, and commercial centers of Southern provincial life, there were few towns, large or small, in the coastal South. So, of course, commercial bakeries such as those that flourished in New Amsterdam by the middle of the 17th century were unknown.

Among the favorite home-baked breads of the Virginia planter families was beaten biscuit, a hotbread made of flour, milk, and shortening. As baking powder did not come into use in the South until after the Revolution, the biscuits had to be made light and fluffy by beating air into the dough mixture rather than by the addition of chemical agents. The traditional way to do this was to toss the biscuit dough onto a smooth-topped tree stump or, in better-equipped kitchens, onto a heavy wooden "biscuit block." It was then whacked hard anywhere from 300 to 500 times with a heavy iron pestle, a flatiron, or the side of a hatchet head.

This task, which often took half an hour or more, required the labor and sole attention of one of the black kitchen slaves, while three or four other cooks put the major parts of the meal together. So, in terms of the labor required, we can say that beaten biscuit was really a luxury food. After the beaten dough had become satiny and blistery with air bubbles, it had to be rolled flat, the biscuits cut out in rounds, their tops pricked with a fork, and then baked. Virginia beaten biscuits were indeed a far cry from the cannonball-like corn dodgers of the North Carolina dirt farmer, and they were delectable when served up hot at the well-burnished dining-room table of the plantation house, to be split, buttered, and devoured with crisp-fried chicken and cream gravy.

Another popular Virginia hotbread was Sally Lunn, which had started out as an almost cakelike bun—yeast-raised and rich with eggs—that was sold by a girl of that name in the famous English spa and resort city of Bath. Those members of the British aristocracy who had frequented the place before becoming Virginia gentlemen farmers had the recipe duplicated in their plantation kitchens, although in the American South Sally Lunn was usually baked in a bread pan and cut into wedges or squares. It was, of course, always eaten hot and well buttered.

An exception to the rule that seemed to dictate cornmeal breads for the poor and wheat-flour breads for the rich was something called Virginia batter bread. A similar hotbread, prepared in the homes of the South Carolina rice- and indigo-plantation owners, was called Carolina egg bread. Both of these were also known, in very similar versions, as "spoon bread" for the simple reason that they were all three soft and puddinglike to the degree that they could not be sliced or even torn apart but actually had to be dug out of the baking dish with a large spoon.

Southern spoon bread is believed to have been derived from *suppawn*, the boiled-milk-and-cornmeal porridge of the New Netherland Dutch. According to one story, *suppawn* became transformed from a porridge to a soft bread when a forgetful cook left it too long on the fire. The porridge crusted on the bottom and the sides, leaving the center, however, still creamy. It tasted so good that someone decided to add eggs the next time. This made the new dish richer and also lighter, especially if the eggs were separated and the whites beaten fluffy with air before being added to the cornmeal mixture.

Actually, the porridgelike but rich and puffy spoon bread was so much like a soufflé that it had to be served very quickly after being removed from the oven lest it fall flat. In the Virginia and Charleston plantation houses, it was hurried along to the table by a relay of servants, to be eaten dripping with melted butter, along with sugar-glazed ham and fresh-cooked greens.

Spoon bread also tastes very good with a beef stew or other gravy-rich meat dish. The bread should be spooned directly onto one's serving plate and immediately dabbed with small pats of butter. The recipe that follows is authentically Southern but is "modernized" with the addition of baking powder so that the bread will remain light and puffed for a little longer after it is taken out of the oven.

✳ SPOON BREAD

1 cup yellow cornmeal
2 cups milk
3 egg yolks
1 cup milk
2 tablespoons butter, melted
3 teaspoons baking powder
1⅛ teaspoons salt
3 egg whites

• Set oven to preheat to 350 degrees Fahrenheit. Remove eggs from refrigerator to allow them to reach room temperature.

• Put cornmeal into a medium-size saucepan. Add the 2 cups of milk, stirring to blend smooth. Cook cornmeal and milk over medium heat, stirring almost constantly, until milk is absorbed and mixture is smooth and porridge-like.

• Carefully separate the eggs, making sure there are no flecks of yolk in the whites. Put the yolks in a medium-size mixing bowl, beat, and add the remaining 1 cup of milk. Beat smooth and add this mixture, stirring constantly, to the cornmeal mixture. Add melted butter, baking powder, and 1 teaspoon of the salt.

• Put the egg whites into a medium-large mixing bowl. Add the remaining ⅛ teaspoon salt and, with a rotary hand beater or an electric beater, beat the whites until they are white and fluffy and will form firm peaks, but are not too dry.

• Slowly add the cornmeal mixture to the egg whites, gently folding and turning it into the whites with a flexible bowl scraper until the two are fairly well blended. Do not overmix or too much air will escape from the beaten egg whites. Carefully turn the mixture into a lightly buttered two-quart casserole dish and bake, uncovered, for 45 minutes or until spoon bread is brown and puffed and feels quite firm to the touch in the center. Serve at once. Makes 6 to 8 servings.

Country Captain
Chicken from the Indies

✳ While the wealth of the Virginia planters sprang from tobacco, that of the South Carolinians resulted largely from rice. By a fortunate circumstance, the English gentlemen who received a land grant from King Charles II and founded Charles Town (later Charleston) in 1680, were presented with a gift of Madagascar seed rice by a grateful sea captain whose storm-damaged ship took refuge in their harbor.

Rice, probably the first to be grown in the New World, did exceptionally well in the Carolina Low Country, which was hot and moist, not unlike the Southeast Asian lands where this grain originated and grew so successfully. Unfortunately, the working conditions in the rice fields were far worse than those in the Virginia tobacco fields, for planting, transplanting, and weeding were backbreaking work that had to be done wading knee-deep in water or sloshing through soupy mud. In addition, there was widespread malaria infestation from the mosquitoes that bred in the coastal marshes. As in Virginia, African slaves were pressed into service, and from their drudgery a thriving plantation economy took hold. In fact, South Carolina continued to be the leading rice producer in North America for the next two hundred years.

A second plantation crop in both South Carolina and Georgia was indigo, a plant from which a much-in-demand blue dye for cloth was extracted. Indigo cultivation was introduced in the 1740s from India where the plant originated and was abundantly grown. In the American South, the preparation of the dye became a plantation industry. This was highly unpleasant because the extraction process produced an evil stench and the dye vats themselves drew and bred swarms of flies and mosquitoes.

The Georgia and South Carolina plantation houses were only a little less grand than those of Virginia. However, as the conditions of the surrounding plantations were often unhealthy or foul-smelling, their owners also maintained tall, airy town houses in Charleston, with tiers of open verandas framed with lacy white trelliswork. In summer, especially, many households moved to Charleston, leaving the fields and dye works to the attentions of their white overseers and black slaves. Charleston was said to be the liveliest of the Southern colonial capitals, with a busy seaport, a brisk commercial life, and a social scene that was a glittering round of dinner parties and balls.

Vendors broke the early morning silence, hawking freshly-caught "she-crab" and "swimpee-raw" from the coastal creeks and inlets, and the house servants hastened to the streets to take in a day's supply for the various dishes that were part of the delicate rice-and-seafood cookery of this part of the lowland South. Being a plentiful local product, rice was used in many kinds of dishes and even appeared in a Charleston bread containing both cooked rice and rice flour, which was known as philpy.

The "wild" foods of the forests, fields, and marshes also found their way into the cooking pots of both rich and poor. In the South, squirrel and rabbit, raccoon and opossum were the basis of a variety of stews. The opossum was known for its habit of playing dead or "playing possum." But when the lucky huntsman could bag one, a favorite dish was "possum 'n' taters"—whole opossum baked with sweet potatoes.

Hogs and chickens were the most prevalent domestic meat animals, so it is not surprising that the two main dishes most closely associated with Southern cooking became ham and fried chicken. Because frying chicken (rather than stewing or roasting it) took so much watching, to make sure each piece came out of the fryer crisp, golden, and evenly cooked, the plantation kitchens probably turned out the best examples of this dish, and the best cream gravy to go with it, in the whole gravy-loving South.

A very different chicken dish was introduced in the South, reportedly at Savannah, Georgia, by the captain of a spice-cargo ship that docked at that coastal center of colonial government. The ship brought with it a whiff of the East—cumin and coriander, cardamom and cloves, turmeric and fenugreek—as well as other exotic curry-powder ingredients. Perhaps it was the ship's captain who taught the preparation of the dish to the kitchen staff of a Georgia planter, or perhaps a Southern gentleman adapted it as the result of travels abroad. In any case, this East Indian-flavored chicken dish with its rich sauce of raisins and almonds, onions and garlic, tomatoes and peppers, was soon being prepared ashore in the lowland South and was being

served with native-grown rice from South Carolina. After a while the sea-borne recipe even began to travel inland, earning for itself the name of Country Captain.

While most cooks in India prepare their own curry powder, skillfully pounding and blending a dozen or more locally obtained spices, commercially-prepared curry powder can be used successfully in this recipe for Country Captain. To give the dish a "hotter" flavor, simply add more curry powder to your taste.

✳ COUNTRY CAPTAIN

 4 tablespoons butter or margarine
 4 tablespoons sliced almonds
 1 medium-size onion, diced into ¼-inch pieces
 1 clove garlic, minced in garlic press or mashed fine
 ½ teaspoon curry powder
 2 tablespoons vegetable oil
10 pieces fryer-chicken parts (legs, thighs, and breasts, in
     any combination), washed and patted dry
     salt and white pepper
 2 cups skinned,* cut-up tomatoes, in large pieces, or 1
     one-pound can tomatoes packed in thick tomato
     purée
 4 tablespoons raisins
 ½ cup green pepper cut in ¼-inch squares
 ½ teaspoon dried thyme

• Melt 2 tablespoons of the butter or margarine in a deep

---

* To skin tomatoes, place whole tomatoes in deep bowl and cover with hot, freshly boiled water. Let stand 5 minutes. Skins will loosen and peel off easily.

10-inch skillet (one that has a cover to fit). Add almonds and sauté, stirring constantly with a wooden spoon, until very pale golden-brown. Remove at once with a slotted spoon and set aside.

• Add 2 more tablespoons of butter or margarine to skillet. Melt, and add the onion, garlic, and curry powder. Cook, stirring, until very lightly browned. Remove with a slotted spoon to a small bowl and set aside.

• Add oil to skillet, heat, and add chicken pieces, skin side down, one layer at a time. Brown on both sides, sprinkling with salt and white pepper. Remove all browned chicken pieces to a large bowl. Add tomatoes to skillet, stirring well with wooden spoon to mix in scrapings from bottom of pan. Add raisins, green pepper, thyme, and onion-garlic-curry mixture. Return chicken pieces, cover skillet, and cook on medium-low heat for about 35 minutes or until chicken is tender. Taste for seasoning, adding more salt and curry powder if desired. Sprinkle almonds atop chicken, heat through, and serve. Boiled white rice and a relish of either sweet, spiced watermelon pickle or Indian mango chutney are very good with Country Captain. Serves 4 to 5.

Short'nin' Bread
The Scots Go South

✳ The large estates of Virginia, Maryland, South Carolina, and Georgia were run, of course, on the almost unseen labors of countless numbers of slaves. So we are not surprised to learn that an 18th-century Virginia gentleman, Robert Beverly, staunchly defended slave-owning. In 1705, in his *History and Present State of Virginia*, Beverly wrote, "I have heard how strangely cruel, and severe, the Service of this Country is represented in some parts of *England* . . . I can assure you with a great deal of Truth, that generally . . . Slaves are not worked near so hard, nor so many Hours in a Day, as the Husbandmen, and Day-Labourers in *England*."

It was true that some plantation owners did restrict their slaves' working day to no more than fifteen hours. But in most cases the purpose was to protect themselves against loss of an investment, through working a slave to death, rather than for any humane or benevolent reasons. It was also true that white indentured servants were sometimes worked even harder than slaves, because their bonded labor (to pay off a sea-passage or other debt) was for a fixed period. But at least these servants became free men and women after a certain number of years, while "the Negroes," as Beverly referred to them, "are call'd Slaves, in respect of the time of their Servitude, because," he added grimly, "it is for Life."

In the North, slavery was accepted in most places almost as matter-of-factly as in the South. Of course, there were fewer slaves because there were fewer large farming estates. Nevertheless, by the first half of the 18th century, one-sixth of the population of Boston consisted of black household and laboring slaves, and almost one-quarter of the population of New York City was black and enslaved. The Quakers and the German religious sects of Pennsylvania were among the few groups clearly opposed to slavery, both in practice and in theory.

As profit was the chief motive of the Southern plantation-owner, the food and clothing provided for his slaves was the cheapest available. An entire category of slave foods came into existence, to be "rediscovered" and given a new recognition in modern, post-slavery America as "soul food." As a fad cuisine, this high-starch, high-fat diet of "fillers" and "leavings" might be temporarily acceptable. But to the many poor whites and poor blacks of the South who subsist on it to this day, it is dull and stodgy at its best, and at its worst malnourishing to the point of producing serious nutritional diseases.

There was nothing very glamorous, in the slave era, about eating hog jowl (pig jaws and cheeks) or hog small intestines. The latter were called chitterlings or "chitlins." For cooking, they were scrubbed as clean as possible, boiled in water to tenderize them, then cut up to oyster size, dipped in meal, and fried in hot lard. The heads, feet, entrails, and other leavings from pig, poultry, or cattle slaughter on the plantation almost always went to the slaves to be cooked and served up at their own tables along with black-eyed peas or hominy grits (coarsely ground hulled corn) and turnip or collard greens.

Foods produced in excess were cheap so, depending on what was plentiful at a given time and place, the slaves might be fed on dried salted fish from New England, molasses from the West Indies, or sweet potatoes, peanuts, and vegetables from the surrounding fields. During the early slave era, diamondback terrapins from the marshy shores of Chesapeake Bay were so numerous that they were fed to Maryland slaves to the point of monotony. But in later years, especially toward the end of the 19th century, these easily-snared salt-water turtles had become so scarce that terrapin soup was a dish commanded only by the most diamond-studded of gourmet diners in fashionable New York and Philadelphia society.

The kitchen-staff slaves of the South were luckier than most because they had the tastings and the leftovers from the dishes that were served to the family and guests in the great house. But these tidbits seldom stretched very far, back in the crowded slave cabins. There were a few slave-food treats, however. One was "cracklin' bread," a cornbread containing bits of pork crackling, the crisp fried bits of skin that floated to the top of the kettle when hog fat was being melted down to make lard.

Another treat was "short'nin' bread," although judging from its expensive ingredients—sugar, butter, and fine wheat flour—this was a very rare and very prized treat indeed. The origin of this rich, crumbly cookie is clear enough, for it was introduced as the traditional "Scotch shortbread" of a group of immigrant Scots weavers who began arriving in the South in 1714.

Prior to coming to the New World, these Scots had lived for some years in Ireland, where they had relocated after leaving Scotland to avoid the high tariffs placed on the hand-woven woolen goods that were their livelihood. When religious persecution began to drive them from Ireland the Scotch-Irish, as they were now known, moved across the Atlantic to Virginia and North Carolina, often making their way westward again a generation or so later, to the North Carolina hill country and to the frontier lands of Kentucky, Tennessee, and West Virginia.

Scotch shortbread—"short" because of the large propor- tion of butter in the recipe, and "bread" because it was not particularly sweet—seemed to travel along with the Scots wherever they went in the American South, and except for the use of brown sugar rather than white, the recipe changed very little. In fact, its popularity spread so quickly that some time in the years soon after the Scots went south, we find the following ditty set to music turning up in Virginia, celebrating one of the good uses to which "shortening," or "short'nin'," bread can be put:

> *Three little children, lying in bed,*
> *Two were sick and the other most dead!*
> *Sent for the doctor, the doctor said:*
> *"Feed these children on short'nin' bread."*
>
> *Mamma's little baby loves short'nin', short'nin',*
> *Mamma's little baby loves short'nin' bread.*
> *Mamma's little baby loves short'nin', short'nin',*
> *Mamma's little baby loves short'nin' bread!*

Whether "Mamma's little baby" was a slave child, a child of one of the modest dirt farmers of the lowland South or the inland hill country, or a white plantation child cared for by a motherly black nurse, here is the recipe for short'nin' bread, the "cake" of the Southern poor and the delight of anyone—Scottish, American, or otherwise—who has ever tasted it.

✳ SHORT'NIN' BREAD

2 cups sifted flour
½ teaspoon salt
½ cup light brown sugar
1 cup chilled sweet butter (½ pound; 2 sticks)

• Set oven to heat to 350 degrees Fahrenheit.

• After measuring out the 2 cups of sifted flour, add the salt and sift again into a large mixing bowl. Add brown sugar, which should be free of lumps and should be measured by pressing it down firmly in measuring cup. Cut butter into chunks and add it to flour mixture.

• Using a pastry blender or two sharp knives worked in a crisscross motion, cut in the butter until it is about the size of peas. Now, with the fingertips, work the butter into the flour until the entire mixture becomes perfectly smooth and comes away cleanly from the sides of the bowl.

• Place the shortbread dough in an ungreased 9 x 9 x 2 baking pan, and press it down evenly and smoothly so that it is the same thickness throughout. With a fork, prick the dough all over. Bake for 20 to 25 minutes, or until shortbread is light brown and stands away slightly from the sides of the pan. Remove from oven and, while still warm, cut shortbread into 1½-inch squares. Cool thoroughly and store in a tightly covered tin. Makes 36 pieces of short'nin' bread.

Tipsy Squire
A Trifle from Britain

✳ Tippling, the drinking of alcoholic beverages on a fairly regular basis, was an activity in which most American colonists indulged. This custom, of course, had its origins in Europe. Water was not always fit to drink, milk was often from tubercular cows or otherwise contaminated, tea and coffee had to be imported from China and Arabia and were costly. Beer, on the other hand, could be brewed from barley or other local grains and European-grown hops. It was cheap, safe, and fairly long-keeping. Wines and distilled liquors, such as gin and brandy, were more intoxicating and even less subject to spoilage.

In addition, alcohol was useful, externally, as an antiseptic, and in an age when effective anesthetic drugs and gases were unknown, alcohol was the balm of the injured and the solace of the sick and dying. It dulled the bite of unbearable pain and made necessary surgery such as amputations possible by reducing the brain-damaging shock that often killed the patient.

In the New World, especially, alcohol braced one against cold and dampness and eased the rigors of outdoor life. So we are not surprised to learn that beer came to New England on the *Mayflower* or that it was the breakfast drink of children in New Netherland. Beer was one of the reasons the colonists began to plant barley in the very early days of settlement. And by 1640, New England (where even Puritan families started the day with a bracing draft of beer all around the table) had its first licensed, commercial breweries.

Once apple orchards got started, the colonists all along the eastern seaboard began to build cider presses for making apple cider. Occasionally it was of the "sweet" or unfermented variety, as innocent as apple juice, but more often they made "hard" cider, a fermented type that could be distilled to a high degree of potency and was very intoxicating. An alcoholic cider was made from pears, too, and was known as perry. The colonists also followed the British tradition of fermenting honey with yeast to make a drink called mead or metheglin. And, of course, once New England sea captains got into the West Indian molasses trade, rum distilleries sprang up in Massachusetts and Rhode Island.

New England rum, however (like the cheap, crude gin of Britain and Holland), was considered the drink of seafarers and the rougher sorts of travelers, including frontier scouts and groups of men on hunting or fishing expeditions. The New Netherland Dutch broke out cases of imported wine or brandy on those special occasions such as weddings and housewarmings when the everyday beer and cider did not seem festive enough. But it was the wealthy Southern planters who were the most lavish importers of fine European wines and brandies.

The growing of wine grapes had been tried in the early days at Jamestown, using both native wild stock and imported vines, but the vineyards had failed to produce a palatable wine. So Virginia aristocrats, like William Byrd II, stocked their cellars with Spanish sherries, wines from Spain's Canary Islands, and with fine Portuguese Madeira. Almost every meal was a festive coming-together at which guests were present and bottles of wine and brandy were poured. In fact, Southern hospitality was so generous that the few innkeepers who tried to maintain establishments in the South complained that they lacked sufficient business because the plantations wined, dined, and slept so many of their would-be customers.

In the great houses of Virginia, sherry, brandy, and Madeira also went into milk punches and fruit punches, as well as into wine jellies and crocks of brandied preserved fruits known as tutti-frutti. The brandy bottle was passed slowly over the mixing bowl in the preparation of George Washington cake, a very large and impressive fruit cake, and of Virginia poundcake, a butter-rich marvel of light, moist tenderness that required at least an hour of vigorous beating to incorporate air into the batter. English desserts like plum pudding were both made and flamed with brandy, while trifle, an English puddinglike concoction of cake slices, fruit preserves, and custard, often concealed a lacing of sherry surreptitiously drizzled over the cake to moisten it.

Trifle looked especially innocent because of the pale, wholesome egg-and-milk custard that masked the dessert. It was said that persons who wished to appear to be teetotalers, such as parsons and other members of the clergy, did their tippling by means of the sherry in the trifle, and so this dish was sometimes called Tipsy Parson. At other times, it was called Tipsy Squire, although we know that few of the wealthy rural squires of the American South bothered to conceal their fondness for imbibing.

As time passed, however, the abundance of fresh, pure water in the New World did cause some people to begin to frown on tippling, and efforts were made by members of polite society to lessen their consumption of alcohol or at least partially to conceal it. Tea-drinking grew very popular as Americans began to import the China-grown leaf for "the cup that cheers but does not inebriate."

Tea, in fact, might have become the most popular non-alcoholic beverage in present-day America if not for the hated British-imposed Townshend Acts of 1767. They included a levy on tea entering American ports and contributed to colonial unrest leading to such Revolution-ary-eve episodes as the Boston Tea Party of 1773. Oddly enough, although we always think of the British as confirmed tea-drinkers, coffee was a more popular drink in 18th-century London than was tea. After the introduction of the tea tax in the American colonies, it became unpatriotic to drink tea, and the colonial taste also turned to coffee, which was to become the staple hot beverage of the new nation after the Revolutionary War.

Probably the only beverage of the colonial era that could be said to be truly American in origin was one developed by the frontier settlers of the inland South. Cut off from the coast, the pioneer farmers of the Kentucky and Tennessee hill country learned to distill a whiskey from corn, for this native American crop grew better than the barley required for beer and faster than the apple trees essential for the making of cider. Corn whiskey was made at home in rude mountain stills. It was good for snakebite and toothache, for the dressing of injuries against infection, and of course as an internal antidote against cold and the grim, hard life of the frontier cabin. Today most American corn whiskeys go by the name of bourbon, for Bourbon County, Kentucky, where much of it was originally made.

It was a far cry from the modestly intoxicating Tipsy Squire of the Virginia Tidewater gentry to the throat-searing "corn likker," tossed down in a single gulp, of the Kentucky mountain folk. But the country was moving forward and change, often brutal and jarring, was in the air. The links with Britain that bound so many of the early colonists by custom and tradition were being rapidly broken as the years of the American Revolution approached.

The following recipe for Tipsy Squire, a trifle from Britain, is a gentle and persuasive reminder of English country life transferred to the plantations of pre-Revolutionary Virginia. It is still an excellent dish today, particularly as a magical means of using up leftover sponge cake and, in so doing, creating a wholly new dessert.

✳ TIPSY SQUIRE

6 ounces (approximately) day-old sponge cake
¼ cup sweet sherry wine (optional)
2 cups milk
3 eggs*
¼ cup sugar*
¼ teaspoon salt*
½ cup thick cherry or strawberry preserves

* If desired, omit these ingredients and combine milk with one package egg-custard pudding mix, cooking according to directions on package, and cooling custard 5 minutes before pouring onto cake slices in bowl.

• Line bottom and sides of a deep one-quart glass bowl or pudding or casserole dish with strips of sponge cake, cut about ½-inch thick. (Reserve sufficient cake strips for two layers to be added later in recipe.) Sprinkle cake slices with a little of the sherry.

• Heat the 2 cups of milk in the top of a double boiler, but over direct heat, until it is scalded (tiny bubbles will form around the rim), watching it carefully as milk must not boil. In a medium-size mixing bowl, beat eggs, add sugar, and salt, and beat well. Add hot milk, a little at a time, beating constantly. Return entire mixture to double-boiler top, place over double-boiler bottom containing hot but not boiling water, and cook for about 8 minutes, or until custard takes on body and is just thick enough to coat a spoon (custard must *not* become *very* thick). Remove custard from heat and cool for about 5 minutes.

• Pour about one-third of the custard over the cake in the bowl, top with a layer of cake strips, sprinkle with a little more sherry, and dab with almost half of the preserves. Add another third of the custard, the last of the cake strips, the rest of the sherry, the rest of the jam, and finally the remainder of the custard. Cool and refrigerate. Serve Tipsy Squire well chilled, spooning it into dessert dishes and topping portions with heavy cream or whipped cream, if desired. Serves 5 to 6.

After the Revolution

Change, movement, the opening up of new frontiers . . . these were the very nature of colonial American life. Even before the colonies went to war to separate themselves politically from England, new developments were rapidly taking place within them.

Already many New Englanders had abandoned their stony-soiled hillside farms for fishing and whaling, trading and lumbering, to be followed after the Revolution by the growth of shipbuilding and of industries such as textile weaving and shoe manufacturing.

The Atlantic-seaboard cornfields and wheatfields began to move farther and farther west to accommodate the nation's growing appetite, and the Middle Atlantic cities of New York and Philadelphia became brisk young centers of banking and commerce, intellectual and cultural activity.

Only the German religious groups of southeastern Pennsylvania, made up of stalwart settlers and model farmers who practiced soil fertilization and crop rotation, kept firmly to their original holdings, preserving their green and fertile pockets of agricultural land despite the shifting patterns around them.

In the coastal South, where the plantation owners tended to be as ruthless with the elements of the soil as with the energies of their slave laborers, the years following the Revolutionary War saw many of the worn-out Tidewater tobacco lands left to revert to wilderness. Plantation owners simply invested their fortunes farther inland (cotton became the large-scale plantation crop after the invention of the cotton gin in 1793) or went into other enterprises. Many of the small dirt farmers of Virginia and the Carolinas worked their stakes on an even more temporary basis. For there was always a new frontier beyond the next range of mountains that promised (but did not necessarily yield) less work with greater rewards.

The whole thrust of American life, for good reasons and for bad, was westward. And of course colonial recipes traveled along with the rolling wagons. Not long after the Revolution, johnnycake was turning up in Ohio, Indiana, and Illinois, snickerdoodles in Kentucky and Missouri, hush puppies in Mississippi, and short'nin' bread in Arkansas.

Meantime, the "first frontier," the eastern seaboard, was becoming the scene of a new culinary ferment, as growing waves of immigrants, both settling and passing through, brought their own Old World traditions from central and eastern Europe, from Scandinavia and the Mediterranean lands. At the same time, trade and transportation, taste and sophistication, wealth and worldliness increased in the coastal cities of the eastern United States, and by the late 19th century affluent Americans were playing host to celebrated European chefs and sitting down to opulent cuisines, once enjoyed only by members of Europe's royal houses.

The nation had come a long way from its cradle days, when all meals had consisted of basic foods, gathered from field and garden, stream and woodland, simply prepared and often crudely served in homes that were little more than rough shelters in the wilderness.

Yet, it is refreshing to know that we can look around us today—two hundred years and more after the Revolution—examine our past, note how fundamental the colonial era is to so many of our institutions (whether we are speaking of foods and cookery or of the federal Constitution), and appreciate the many ways in which that vital era is reflected in our present.

Index